'Wise insights relating art and religion reward the reader of Graham Howes' fine work. His interdisciplinary integrity stems from a deeply rooted study of both art and theology, which he reveals as twins. He explores sources of creativity in a variety of successful collaborations from Fra Angelico at San Marco to Moore at Northampton, Matisse at Vence, Rothko at Houston, and Viola's videos of *The Passions* and *The Messenger*. Graham Howes helps us see how "faith lives from the particular" incarnation, how concrete projects mediate the transcendent, and how we may hope to hearten religion and art to inspire and to inform each other.'

Douglas G. Adams, Professor of Christianity and the Arts, Pacific School of Religion

'Long involved, internationally, in the study of visual arts and religion, Graham Howes has given us a book that only he could have written. While providing a lucid overview of the multiple connections between visual art and religious belief (or "the sacred"), he also supplies fascinating case studies and attends to pertinent historical and theological developments up to the present moment. It is hard to believe that Howes can condense so much insight and valuable information into such a relatively short book. *The Art of the Sacred* should not be missed by anyone who wants to explore the topic intelligently, or get a real sense of the importance (and complexity) of the issues.'

Frank Burch Brown, Frederick Doyle Kershner Professor of Religion and the Arts, Christian Theological Seminary, Indianapolis

'Now that many visitors to museums and galleries have so little knowledge of the religious subjects painted by artists in the past, Graham Howes' book is superbly well-timed. His illuminating introduction to the aesthetics of art and belief will prove indispensable. Above all, he succeeds in reminding us that great art is essentially an act of faith, Christian or otherwise.'

Richard Cork, art critic, historian and broadcaster

'John Ruskin threw down the gauntlet in *Modern Painters*, 150 years ago: "How far [has] Fine Art, in all or any ages of the world, been conducive to the religious life." Using this famous challenge as his starting point, Graham Howes takes us on a multidisciplinary journey through the changing relationship between aesthetic and religious experience mainly in the Western Church tradition – though with applications beyond – from historical, art historical and sociological perspectives, and with the eye of a trained artist. He writes about a very complex web of ideas in a refreshingly clear and no-nonsense way. Moreover, his selection of illustrative case-studies (among them the mid-Victorians, the clerical patronage of Walter Hussey, the work of Matisse and Rothko, Viola and Gormley, and – for me the most fascinating – the public's reaction to the

'Seeing Salvation' exhibition at London's National Gallery in 2000) is both imaginative and apt. I will treasure for a long time his demolition of fashionable assertions about 'the church as heritage centre'. *The Art of the Sacred* is an excellent introduction to a surprisingly timely subject.'

Sir Christopher Frayling, Rector, Royal College of Art, London

'Graham Howes provides an eminently civilised entry into the range of relationships, historical and contemporary, between art, society and religion. He does so through illuminating case studies and a clear delineation of how things stand today when the keystone of overarching, shared meanings has collapsed. Few scholars are as well placed to articulate the tensions over the last quarter of a millennium, between Art Gallery and Church, Abstraction and Content, Image and Word, the inward and outward explorations of individual artists and the communal discipline of theology.'

David Martin, Emeritus Professor of Sociology,
London School of Economics, University of London

'Spanning centuries of sacred imagery and half a dozen fields of scholarly inquiry, Graham Howes does what few can manage: to condense a dizzying range of thought and art into an eminently sensible, persuasive, and authoritative reflection that will inform specialist and lay reader alike. Drawing on a career of distinguished teaching at Cambridge, Howes writes with enviable clarity and insight about a concentration of intellectual interests that has challenged writers on religion and art for quite some time. By combining extensive knowledge in art history, aesthetics, and theology with a background in sociology and the history of culture, Howes fashions a compelling account of artist, believer, patron, institution, and viewer. This integrative approach not only sheds crucial light on the past, it signals the future of inquiry itself. This book will prove to be singularly important.'

David Morgan, Duesenberg Professor of Christianity
and the Arts, Valparaiso University

'It is sometimes said these days that art galleries are the new cathedrals, or that art is the last refuge of the sacred in our society. In this very lively and accessible book, Graham Howes explores the sense in which this might be true, and the sense in which it leaves the most important questions unanswered. He takes us with sympathy and skill through a number of case studies tracing the interweaving of creativity with patronage and wider cultural trends, and offers a fresh and challenging account of why neither religion not visual art can finally rest in the assumption that the abstract is the ideal. *The Art of the Sacred* makes a genuinely new contribution to a vital debate.'

Rowan Williams, Archbishop of Canterbury

the art of the sacred

an introduction to the aesthetics of art and belief

GRAHAM HOWES

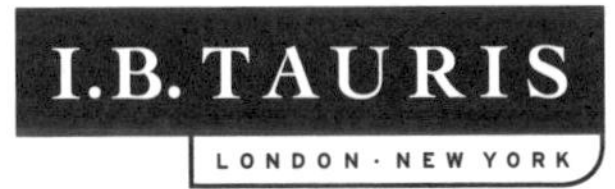

Published in 2007 by
I.B.Tauris & Co. Ltd
6 Salem Rd, London W2 4BU
175 Fifth Avenue, New York NY 10010
www.ibtauris.com

In the United States and Canada distributed by Palgrave Macmillan,
a division of St. Martin's Press, 175 Fifth Avenue, New York, NY 10010

ISBN   978 1 84511 005 5 (Hb)
ISBN   978 1 84511 006 2 (Pb)

A full CIP record for this book is available from the British Library
A full CIP record for this book is available from the Library of Congress
Library of Congress catalog card: available

Typeset in Monotype Jansen by illuminati, Grosmont,
www.illuminatibooks.co.uk
Printed and bound in Great Britain by
T.J. International Ltd, Padstow, Cornwall

contents

preface and acknowledgements

This book has had a long gestation, and its contents reflect an evolving, often serendipitous, preoccupation with aspects of the precise relationship of visual to religious experience, both individually and collectively, within differing cultural and credal contexts. To begin with, as an 18-year-old art student, I swiftly recognised my inability to bridge the gap between my technical shortcomings and my barely sensed interior life. As an undergraduate and postgraduate historian, my strong interest in the Victorians, sharpened successively by Geoffrey Best, John Nurser and Owen Chadwick, focused increasingly on the links between their religion, their art and their architecture. A subsequent academic mutation into a sociologist of religion brought not only the opportunity to reflect more generally on the relationship, past and present, between religious change and the visual arts. It also led to the personal friendship and support of outstanding British scholars such as David Martin, the late Bryan Wilson,

Eileen Barker and Kieran Flanagan, while further afield the late Edward Shils in Chicago, Philip Hammond and the late Ninian Smart in Santa Barbara, Robert Wuthnow at Princeton, David Morgan at Valparaiso, Frank Burch Brown at Virginia Tech, and the late Yoshio Abe in Tokyo provided both unstinting hospitality and the opportunity to try out some of my ideas on others. Three other experiences have been especially formative. One was an invitation from Michael Kitson and Alan Bowness to lecture to their own Courtauld students. Another was working part-time for Robert Runcie at Lambeth Palace at a time when Leonard Rosoman was painting the roof of the Chapel, and sharing some of the artist's own insights and reflections on his task. Third, active involvement with ACE (Art and Christianity Enquiry) both nationally and internationally brought with it a wide network of the like-minded – Tom Devonshire Jones, Charles Pickstone, Allan Doig, Mary Charles Murray, Wilson Yates, John and Jane Dillenberger, Doug Adams, Mark Cazalet and others too numerous to mention. They will know who they are. Finally, I have, over the years, had regular and privileged access to exceptionally alert and responsive students, not only within my own university and college, but also among members of my Continuing Education classes throughout the Cambridge region – especially in Letchworth and Bedford – who have always provided plenty of robust reality-testing for many of my more tentative hypotheses.

More immediate thanks go to my publisher (and former pupil) Alex Wright, who has shown extraordinary forbearance throughout, and to Martin Boycott Brown and Emilie Dyer both of whom have calmly and expertly extricated me from numerous word-processing crises. My biggest personal debt is expressed in the dedication.

*For Shirley
Without whom*

introduction

In 1856 the great Victorian critic John Ruskin asked his readers
'How far has Fine Art, in all or any ages of the world, been
conducive to the religious life?'[1] His question, and its answer,
remains a demanding and difficult one, not least in a world supposedly characterised by major changes in both art and religion,
and where Image often appears to speak louder than Word. This
book tries, therefore, to do three things: to examine the degree
to which aesthetic experience can shape religious experience,
how far the former can reinforce the latter (and vice versa), and
how far such a process can militate against, and perhaps wholly
negate, such experience. These are very complex issues, where,
even if we can pick our way successfully through a crowded
semantic minefield strewn with terms like 'religion', 'theology', 'faith', 'ideology', 'sacred', 'transcendental' and 'spiritual',
two very crude, but necessary, questions remain. What is the
historical evidence for the linkages between religious art and

religious experience, and what is the empirical evidence for the present state of that relationship? I come at both as a historian by training, a sociologist of religion by adoption, and also as an art historian manqué. Attentive, even exasperated, readers will find trace elements of all these disciplines in much of the discussion that follows.

All three disciplines also carry their own limitations. Most sociologists, for example, have tended to shy away from the aesthetic dimensions of religion as either too problematic as hard evidence or as simply too marginal to merit more than a mere footnote. Among the classical sociologists, Max Weber and Georg Simmel are, predictably, the honourable exceptions, with the former regarding religious art itself as a 'social fact', and as virtually axiomatic that traditional Indian art, for example, should reveal many of the basic features of traditional Indian religion, while the latter (himself a Jewish convert to Christianity) could write that 'art empowers the soul to supplement one world with the other and thereby to experience itself at the point of union.'[2] In our own time, David Martin[3] has long been interested in the relationship of sacred music to religious change, while Robert Wuthnow[4] has recently documented how music and art now have an increasingly integral role in the revitalisation of American religion. Social anthropologists, too, taking their cue from the French sociologist Émile Durkheim, have long emphasised the socially integrative role of religious art objects, their explicit functions as an expression of religious beliefs and in generating cosmological perceptions. Particularly relevant here is the increasing attention some anthropologists, notably Anthony Forge and Robert Layton,[5] have paid to the relationship between iconographic change and the 'modernisation' of traditional belief systems.

Similarly, the current generation of social and cultural historians – many of whom draw heavily upon the concepts and techniques of the social sciences – have also had much to offer. The Vovelles,[6] for example, have plotted with great ingenuity and precision the transformations of pictorial representations of death and the afterlife in Provence from the fifteenth century to the present, relating this to disease, shifting theological attitudes, and the 'de-Christianisation' of folk Christianity. In a North American context, Colleen McDannell[7] has fruitfully linked religion and mass consumption through the organising construct of 'material culture', while David Morgan[8] continues to explore the mechanisms whereby religious practices, attitudes and ideas are articulated through religious iconography, thus constituting a whole dynamic of what he calls 'visual piety'.

The same emphasis – on the centrality of art objects to belief and practice, and the relationship of the former to the latter amid processes of cultural and credal change – has long been an active concern of art historians. Some have tended to view this relationship as a 'given', to be presumed rather than proved, but others have increasingly sought to show how the links – institutional, credal and cognitive – between artefact and belief system – are visible and explicit, if also fluid. For example, over ninety years ago, Émile Mâle[9] produced convincing evidence of the precise links between late medieval Christianity, in both its elite and popular forms, and the style and content, and temporal and spatial distribution, of Late Gothic art and architecture. More recently, Andrée Hayum[10] has brilliantly set the Isenheim altarpiece within the liturgical and sacramental economies of early-sixteenth-century German Catholicism, while Joseph Leo Koerner[11] has convincingly demonstrated the links between Lutheran theology and an emergent Protestant aesthetic.

Yet underneath the analytical and investigative strategies of each discipline lie a number of formidable theoretical and technical challenges. One is that in scrutinising religious art in any culture we have to take great care with our assumptions concerning the iconicity of religious symbols and the so-called 'creative' character of visual images. The late Richard Wollheim,[12] for one, has argued persuasively that when we discuss iconicity in any cultural setting we have to take account of the relation of the sign to the sign-user as well as the referent. It is, he says, 'as and when signs become for us "fuller" objects that we may also come to feel that they have greater appropriateness to their referent.' The problem, of course, is just how to tease this kind of sense data from those who encounter – physically, emotionally and intellectually – religious art, in whatever form or tradition.

A second problem is that there are real difficulties in distinguishing between religious art as a set of symbols giving information about the content and place of religion in a society irrespective of individuals' interest in or proximity to it, and the same art functioning for *individuals* within that society.

Third, there is the difficulty – by no means confined to anthropologists studying less developed societies – of distinguishing between the physical representation of the sacred as an art product and as a cult object – a problem which is particularly acute when the reproduction process of such objects is speeded up. Images of Mexico's 'Our Lady of Guadalupe' are one such example, and what African retailers often call 'airport art' another. Finally there is the 'traditional' descriptive difficulty of whether or not to regard religious art – along with religion or art itself – as a free-standing, autonomous, category of ideas and experience, or essentially as no more than the visual spin-off from political, social, cultural and institutional activity. With such difficulties in mind I want to identify four distinct dimensions to the relationship between religious art, religious belief and religious experience. I will label them (i) *iconographic*, (ii) *didactic*, (iii) *institutional*, and (iv) *aesthetic*. Although they are historically and culturally inseparable – converging and diverging, fusing and differentiating within and across the major religious traditions, and sometimes beyond them – they are regarded as analytically separable for the purposes of the extended discussion that is the focus of the first chapter.

I

four dimensions of religious art

the iconographic dimension

In religious art, as well as in everyday language, icons are images of saints or holy personages. The icon is not simply a useful adjunct to worship but a vital element in it. Within the Christian Orthodox tradition especially, an icon painter's execution is not an assertion of his own individuality, but a magical act. He (rarely she!) is setting up a field within which powerful forces can operate. If he strays too far, then the magic will not happen. The icon (*Figure 1*) is a symbol which so participates in the reality it symbolises that it is itself worthy of reverence. It is an agent of the Real Presence. In this sense the icon is not a picture to be looked at, but a window through which the unseen world looks onto ours. As the eighth-century theologian John of Damascus put it, icons 'contain a mystery and, like a sacrament, are vessels of divine energy and grace.... Through the intermediary of sensible perception our minds receive a spiritual impression and are uplifted towards the invisible divine majesty.'[1] Today, the Orthodox Church regards icons as one form of revelation and knowledge of God and as one means of communication with Him. As channels of grace like the cross and the Gospels, icons are sacramental, different from ordinary material objects yet *not* in themselves holy. The icon both depicts and shares in the sanctity and glory of its prototype and is thus worthy to receive *proskynesis*, veneration, but not *latreia*, adoration, which is reserved for God alone.

Yet, as social anthropologists like Campbell[2] and Kenna[3] have shown, when Orthodox theologians' pronouncements and the sentiments and behaviour of many devout Greek peasants are taken together, discrepancies become apparent. The peasants do not seem to recognise the theologians' injunction that the icon as a channel of grace is not powerful in itself and must not be treated as such. 'Escalation' occurs, and they certainly speak of and act towards the icons as if they *were* powerful in themselves. The tissues and pieces of cotton wool with which the church icons are dusted are kept for amulets and for use in the household cult of icons. Furthermore, neither Orthodox theologians nor social anthropologists can really tell us precisely *why* one icon is regarded as more powerful than another. Campbell, for example, tells us that the Saraktasani, transhumant shepherds of north-west Greece, insist that 'with respect to the relation of one saint to the many icons of that saint ... one revelation is more efficient than another', but the shepherds 'do not explain how or why'. Campbell's own comment goes a little further:

'in these ideas we see the refraction which even divine energy suffers when it enters the material and sensible world'.[4] But it is surely not enough in itself to say that divine power is refracted. Why is it focused in some material objects and not in others, and why concentrated more in some of these and not in others?

The second issue here is a theological – or rather a Christological – one, namely the idea of man as made in the image of God. The classic example of this is the iconoclastic controversy of the eighth and ninth centuries. The iconoclasts objected to any attempt to portray Christ on the grounds that to do so would be to presuppose that he was only a human being. His divine nature would be ignored (since representation of this was impossible) and this would be a most misleading way of representing the God-man. The opponents of the iconoclasts, the iconophiles, defended the practice of painting Christ on the grounds that this was the obvious way of taking the Incarnation seriously. For them, not to seek to embody Christ in a picture or sculpture betrayed a residual disbelief in the genuine historicity and humanity of Christ. In this sense the controversy was supra-aesthetic. It was about something crucial to Christian belief – the reality of the Incarnation. In the end the iconophiles won the day, and with them also triumphed the theology which they had developed. It was the Incarnation that legitimated Early Christian art, making possible the visualisation of God. Yet out of this clash came not only what Ladner has called 'two normative approaches to the human body – the incarnational and the spiritualized'[5] – which have been in tension throughout

Christian history, but also two attitudes towards the arts which have played a dominant role in church – and art – history ever since.

The conflict re-emerged, and was re-enacted, early in the Protestant Reformation. Its outcome was in one sense a victory, albeit a pyrrhic one, of the verbal over the visual. If Catholicism had set up images as bridges between God and man, Protestantism burned them all, and there was no going back. Indeed, as Hans Belting has written, 'the empty walls of the reformed churches were visible proof of the idolatrous images of the papists. They attested to a purified *desensualised* religion that now put its trust in the Word.'[6] Protestantism reified language as the means of linking Man to God. Yet the historical reality was far more complex. For example, Luther himself promulgated what amounted to a cognitive and credal interdependence between word and image, while for Calvin the only *visual* symbolisation of the divine was the Eucharist. To make material images of the uncircumscribable, all-creating Creator, whose real images were already around us in the form of fellow creatures and also present at the Eucharist itself, was evident idolatry. Zwingli, in his turn, argued that 'images are not to be endured, for all that God has forbidden, there can be no compromise.'[7]

The motives for, and the enactment of, iconoclastic acts within local communities was even more variegated. For example, as Wandel has so vividly documented, in Zurich the 'idols' were deemed voracious, 'stealing food and heat from needy human beings, the "true images of God"', while in Strasbourg most iconoclastic acts linked images to altars, attacking both for their role in a ritual context that evangelical preachers and citizens regarded as 'idolatrous' and 'blasphemous' and where the laity had – both literally and metaphorically – no place. In Basle, on the other hand, iconoclastic acts were directed at images that seemed to symbolise a formal division between the 'spiritual' clergy and the 'carnal' laity – a division that 'denied the status of laity the same quality of piety it attributed to clergy'. In England, however, as Eamon Duffy has so meticulously documented, the 'stripping of the altars', especially between 1547 and 1553, was not merely perceived as a specifically Protestant religious act, but also as an institutionalised act of state. At its heart 'was the necessity of destroying, of cutting, hammering, scraping or melting into a deserved oblivion the monuments of popery, so that the doctrines they embodied might be forgotten.'[8] Such attempts at the physical erasure of collective memory are, of course, permanent features of political as well as religious history – from the refashioning of some churches into 'temples of reason' in post-revolutionary France, to the literal and symbolic toppling of statues of Josef Stalin and Saddam Hussein in our own time.

In any case, there is substantial historical evidence of a genuinely religious art which does *not* set out to be iconic; its function is different though not unrelated. 'I want to paint man and woman', wrote Van Gogh, 'with that something of the eternal which the halo used to symbolise, but which we now seek to confer through the actual radiance of our colour vibrations'.[9] Even more self-evidently, the work of a Rembrandt (especially, perhaps, in his etchings), or nearly all of Rouault, may achieve something of what the icon achieves, but its function is still other. It may set out to enflesh and communicate a transfigured and transfiguring Christian vision, but it is not explicitly liturgical and ecclesiastical in character. Indeed it could even be argued that Western Christianity has largely abandoned formally iconic art since about 1300, since the intimate union of visual art with liturgy, which survives in the Eastern tradition, has never been entirely taken for granted in Western Europe – especially where Protestantism has predominated – and has lived on only in a very debased form, if at all. Hence the key question here is not only the perennial one about the nature of the liturgy itself, but also whether the partial divorce between visual art and liturgy has necessarily been an unmitigated disaster for the Christian (and secular) imagination of the West. Such a debate should itself proceed, as Rowan Williams once reminded us, beyond the simple fallacy which deduces the proposition 'all art should be liturgical' from the proposition 'all liturgy should be artistic'.[10]

the didactic dimension

Both art and theology have been described as 'raids on the inarticulate' in their attempts to extend the basic experience of faith into new fields. In the Latin West, as opposed to the orthodox East, Ruskin's leading question (cited at the outset of this book) as to 'how far has Fine Art, in all or any ages of the world, been conducive to the religious life?' remains a pertinent and perennial one. Ruskin's own point of reference was, of course, European Gothic art and architecture of the twelfth and thirteenth centuries, where both served as powerful didactic instruments. Indeed as early as 1005 a local synod at Arras had already proclaimed that 'art teaches the unsettled what they cannot learn from books'. Two centuries later we find Bonaventure defining the visual not only as an open scripture made visible through painting, for those who were uneducated and could not read, but also as an aid to 'the sluggishness of the affections … for our emotion is aroused more by what is seen than by what is heard',[11] and the transitory nature of human memory is such that 'the things we have seen remain with us more than things we have heard'.

The aesthetic consequences of these assumptions are to be found in many decorative schemes – from the crudest Doom painting above the chancel arch of a remote rural church to the elaborate sculptural programmes of Chartres or Lincoln. Yet recent scholarship has increasingly underlined the degree to which the Gothic was designed to function as more than a mere visual aid. It also served as a medium for religious insight and spiritual awareness, with a specifically sacramental function in the worship of God. This was especially the case with the interior space of many French Gothic cathedrals. There, as the famous Abbot Suger of St Denis in Paris (*Figure 2*), described it:

> I see myself dwelling in some strange region of the universe
> which neither exists entirely in the slime of the earth nor
> entirely in the purity of heaven; and that, by the Grace of God,
> I can be transported from this inferior to that higher world in
> an anagogical manner … transferring that which is material to
> that which is immaterial.[12]

In other words, the building itself had the capacity to lead the mind from the world of appearances to the contemplation of the divine order, and to render spiritual things visible. Yet we also know, especially from Suger himself, that French cathedral Gothic was also felt to be just as important for its technical excellence, as a feat of engineering and intellect, as it was for its spiritual and culturally reflexive qualities. Here God – the architect of the universe – was worshipped most highly in his attributes of light, measure and number. In this sense there is nothing mysterious about the unparalleled success of Gothic, for, as Heer describes it 'a new technique and a new approach to art were yoked to a spiritual vision heavily preoccupied with "technology", mathematics and geometry'.[13] Yet it could be argued that, at the same time, the initially didactic functions of such religious art were, in a sense, being intellectualised, even secularised. Such art was in truth designed to instruct all believers, but how far was it made for the believer and how far for the God whom that believer worshipped? William Golding's novel *The Spire* illuminates this issue – the unstable equilibrium between the didactic and the sacramental – with power and insight. How far was his Dean Jocelin's cathedral to serve primarily as a sermon in stone or as a gratuitous act of faith? What mattered more in it, the worshipper or the worshipped?

Similar tensions are to be found elsewhere in the history of Christian art, and most notably perhaps in the relationship between Catholic doctrine and Baroque art and architecture during the Counter-Reformation and its colonial aftermath. The rationale for such a relationship was perhaps threefold. One was that art could serve as a means of reasserting orthodox Christian dogma to Catholic elites already overexposed to both the secular humanism and pagan mythologies that pervaded Renaissance life, art, and thought. The second was that, as St Basil had put it over twelve hundred years earlier, 'artists do as much for religion with their pictures as the orators do with their eloquence'.[14] Hence their role in responding to the specific injunction of the Council of Trent to reform and reinvigorate the Catholic Church using art as a vehicle – while also visually reaffirming Roman *auctoritas* – was perceived as a potentially important one. Finally, in direct opposition to Protestant teaching, and Protestantism's whitewashed, minimalist aesthetic, Counter-Reformation Catholicism fostered the creation and veneration of images by formally proclaiming that the aim of art was to induce men to piety and bring them to God. Hence, while not suggesting that Counter-Reformation art is synonymous with Baroque art (indeed the former precedes the latter by over half a century), both were heavily committed – in a manner Suger would have found wholly familiar – to an overtly didactic visual theology.

This was expressed in a variety of ways. One was to use art to create or recover the lost or diminished sense of the holy. The means were to strive for what Argan has called 'a sacred theatricality', whereby the exterior or even more the interior of Baroque churches – whether in Venice or Vierzehnheiligen – became a glorious forecourt to Heaven. Indeed, as Argan perceptively comments,

the very fact that the declared aim of Baroque poetics was
the 'marvellous', which implies the suspension of the intellectual faculty, demonstrates in what zones of the human mind
propaganda was to act through the image – on the imagination
in fact, considered as the source and the impulse of feelings,
which in their turn were to be forced into action.[15]

In modern terminology such a cognitive strategy – familiar to
Bernini and his contemporaries as 'hearing through the eyes'
– could be described as aiming at a 'subliminal' level of communication, where visual images have an auxiliary, instrumental
function. In the Gesu in Rome, for example, the intellectual
unity of the iconography, spreading from chapel to chapel and
nave to nave, and emulated in the spatial and spiritual unity
of the architecture, attempted, in Howard Hibbard's phrase,
'to furnish a progressive religious experience for those who
entered'.[16] Once inside, especially when gazing upwards at Gaulli's 'The Adoration of the Holy Name of Jesus' on the ceiling
(*Figure 3*), one does not remain a passive observer, but becomes
an active participant in the religious drama itself. At the same
time, if two major transformations in the concept of religious
art between the sixteenth and seventeenth centuries were from
contemplation to excitation, and from narrative to propaganda,
the third – epitomised in the Gesu itself – was a built form that
fitted a new conception of piety. In the simplicity of a single
nave the faithful could receive the full impact of the preacher's
words and easily follow the ceremonies in the short apse which
replaced the long and complex choir of the Gothic cathedral.
'For 'even in our churches' said Oliva, the Jesuit Vicar-General
in 1664, 'we do not go beyond certain limits of extent and height

which put obstacles in the way of our preachers and interfere with the devotion of our visitors'.[17] There were limits, too, on the form and subject matter of painting and sculpture within. As Howard Hibbard has clearly documented, it is certain that the Church authorities

> had a firm and measurable hold on what they wanted to be represented in their churches. The lives and miracles of their saints as well as their dogmatic beliefs had to be illustrated and this task could not, of course, be handled by the artists without programmes prepared for them by learned clerics.[18]

The decorative schema of the Gesu's own chapels exemplifies such a process at work. It proceeds like a sermon from anecdotal references to this world and its ills, goes on to invoke the joyous birth and triumphant sacrifice of the living Christ, and finally offers a meditation on heaven and its ineffable mysteries. The clear pattern and progressive development of the theme is unfolded and elaborated like a sermon, with parallels of Old and New Testaments, of ancient and modern, and most particularly with examples from the lives of the saints and the invocation of Mary as intercessor. The medium is essentially subordinate to the message.

Yet uniformly didactic intentions did not necessarily lead, even when Jesuit-directed, to monolithic homogeneity in the style and content of Baroque religious art and architecture. True, with the latter, every structural element had an allegorical as well as a spatial meaning. The pilasters and columns allude to the sustaining power of the faith, but also – like the Gothic – demonstrate its truth by creating a space calculated to impress on the faithful an ideal image of the order of the universe. Similarly, most Baroque altarpieces, laden with images and symbols, not only played a similar role to that which in medieval cathedrals belonged to the doorway, but also articulated the kind of Christ-centred devotion reborn in the Counter-Reformation, where so many statues of saints point, by their position, look and demotic gesture, exclusively towards the altar. The statues themselves, in both public and domestic settings, are part of what Argan calls 'the defence and revaluation of images … the great undertaking of the Baroque age'[19] whereby the Church reaffirmed the validity of visual rhetoric as a means of persuasion. Hence it encouraged the most spectacular forms of art, just as it accentuated the spectacular character of worship and ritual. 'Art', in its widest sense, became an essential element in a new kind of personal religious engagement, where the interdependence of devotional praxis and private belief was regarded as axiomatic.

The aesthetic consequences were more variegated than is sometimes assumed. Best known was what Émile Mâle has called 'the new realism',[20] whereby artists, still firmly within ecclesiastical guidelines, were permitted, even encouraged, to express themselves with freedom and intensity, so long as the work of art was genuinely religious in intent. Emotional and spiritual intensity were meant to be felt. Figures of saints, for example, unlike many of their Gothic or Renaissance proto-types, are, as Martin puts it, 'far from being disembodied spirits [but] people living in crisis, divinely touched yet living in the flesh, aware of the earth and of their inward experience'.[21] A second category of Baroque religious art was the product of that Counter-Reformation Quietism (itself essentially Spanish in origin) which emphasised the possibility of direct contact between the dedicated individual soul and the voice of God under conditions of spiritual quietude and passive receptivity. Its artistic expression – exemplified by Zurbaran – was essentially restrained, ascetic, and lacking in colour, movement or overt drama. A third, wholly contrasting, didactic strategy is exemplified in Gaulli's ceiling for the Gesu. Here, described in detail by Hibbard,

> between the physical space, the allegorical space, and the symbolical space, is a continuity and a progression as between terrestrial life and life beyond the earth. This is the thesis of communication, or of the 'ladder' which St Francis of Sales opposed to the Protestant thesis of man's utter inability to communicate with God.[22]

The same fresco also carries another, more triumphalist message. To cite Hibbard again,

> Gaulli uses the abstract symbol of Christ's monogram as a source of physical light and extends the space of the church into the painted sky, which is filled with angels and saints. He is trying to show that this miraculous mission is the logical sequel of the continuous miracle of Providence operating on earth through the medium of the Church.[23]

Throughout Catholic Europe, and beyond, in the pagan and recently converted countries of the New World – and especially in Mexico, Brazil and Peru – the dual messages of the Christian story and the power and authority of the Catholic Church were continuously articulated, affirmed and expressed by artist, architect and craftsman alike.

Today such overtly visual didacticism is rare, and often in reverse, especially within Western Christianity. While many can, at least in theory, read scripture, relatively few can 'read' paintings or stained-glass windows, and most recent revivals of faith and devotion – for example, Liberation Theology or Charismatic Renewal movements – have tended to be grounded in words rather than pictures. Indeed among many cultural and ecclesiastical elites the presumption is usually that while religious art may have some didactic, even aesthetic, value, it has no cognitive function. It is useful for those, especially the very young, who cannot read, and need pictures, but not for those who have mastered discursive reasoning and the manipulation of abstractions: these have no need of the image. For, as an Anglican bishop, the late John Tinsley, once remarked, 'Christians have surrendered with amazing ease to the notion that the image is a lesser form of truth than the concept, as if image and concept were alternative ways of saying the same thing, except that the image helps those who have more imagination than logic.' 'One can', he continues, detect 'a secret preference for language, words, speech, writing, as the appropriate and only satisfactory way of expressing theological truths and communicating the Gospel'.[24] Yet the central question remains. It is whether art is a way of seeing and knowing which is as truth-bearing in its way as philosophical and scientific method. It is unsurprising, therefore, that as institutions the Christian churches have so often shown a marked ambivalence in their attitude to the arts. This ambivalence is the focus of the next section.

the institutional dimension

As we have seen, the art-historical evidence clearly reveals that for many centuries religious institutions served as relatively undemanding patrons of religious art because they had not, until relatively recently, felt it necessary to demand 'sincerity' from the artist. In medieval society, as in many primitive societies, they could take his work for granted. Essentially, in Riesman's phrase, 'tradition-directed',[25] the artist did not have to worry about 'feeling': he was given his assignment – his Crucifixion or his Virgin – and knew perfectly well, down to the last gesture and the last fold of drapery, what he had to do. The religious form was accepted by both parties. This institutional framework continued to function and to provide an adequate reference point for the artist long after he had ceased to take it for granted that the chief part of his work would be religious and long after he had developed sufficient spiritual autonomy to acquire a quite personal notion of sacred art. In the fifteenth century, for example, the Church seems to have found no difficulty in accepting sacred art that was overtly frivolous and worldly in treatment, and, in the High Renaissance, as Edgar Wind[26] has so vividly shown, paganism established a comfortable modus vivendi with Christianity. It was not until after the Counter-Reformation that the Inquisition raised some objections to Veronese's translation of the New Testament into both the proud and flaunting opulence and seedy lowlife of contemporary Venice, and even this was a relatively unemphatic protest. Later still, Poussin's highly formalised neoclassical treatment of biblical themes was perceived in ecclesiastical circles as essentially 'High' Art rather than 'Sacred' Art per se – a reclassification of the genre that continued well into the mid-nineteenth century.

How radical such a mutation was may be judged from the fact that from the mid-nineteenth century, a period in which many exceptional artists flourished and in which many were intensely religious, there is hardly one instance of a great master (except perhaps Delacroix) being asked to decorate a church. As far as Impressionism is concerned, and also with German and American Expressionism, for the first time in history, great aesthetic movements largely developed without at any point making contact with organised religion. Indeed if one were to write a history of religious art in the last hundred years or so it might be summarised as the virtual extinction of such art as a significant activity by significant artists. There are, of course, as we shall see later, some significant exceptions – Matisse's Vence Chapel, Rothko's chapel at Houston, Sutherland's 'Christ in Glory' in Coventry Cathedral, and Moore's 'Madonna and Child', at St Matthew's, Northampton, spring immediately to mind – but in general it would appear that many of the works of greatest interest today, from both an artistic and a religious point of view, are works executed by artists, spontaneously and independently, outside the churches, and commissioned entirely for themselves. Picasso's 'Guernica' and Dalí's 'Christ of St John of the Cross' are the most self-evident examples.

A third, important category (and one which recurs throughout art history) are those works commissioned by religious bodies but ultimately rejected by them as somehow lacking in some important respect from the point of view of their faith. Assy,[27] in Eastern France, is a revealing case. There, over ten years, from 1937 onwards, a church was constructed and decorated largely through the stimulus of a French Dominican, and former painter, Father Couturier, who knew many leading artists personally and persuaded them to collaborate in a large enterprise of religious painting, sculpture, stained glass and tapestry. His idea of commissioning certain well-known artists who were not themselves primarily interested in religious art, for a project of religious decoration and expression, met with great resistance within the French Catholic Church. Its main objection to this kind of art was not that those who executed them were atheists or communists (although some in fact were both) or that their perceptions of religious themes were sometimes – literally and metaphorically – sketchy. It was rather the perception that such artists would be unable, because of their commitment to a modern style of art, to approximate to an idiom of religious art that had arisen under very different cultural and credal conditions and that had its own established values and traditions of representation and symbolism. For example, it was objected that 'Christ on the Cross' by Germaine Richier (*Figure 4*) 'suggested nothing of redemption or of the spiritual meaning of Christ's suffering upon the Cross'. Similarly, it was said that the work of Rouault 'was itself so ugly that it would evoke in the pious observer a disturbing sense of the body in its deformation rather than transmit a spiritual message'. It's interesting to note here that Rouault, one of the few painters of the twentieth century who was a conventionally religious man, and who almost alone among the advanced painters of his time continuously represented religious themes, especially from the life of Christ, received no formal recognition from his own church except from isolated individuals. On the other hand, Cézanne, who in the last fifteen years of his life was a faithful churchgoer, never undertook a religious theme. Hence on the one hand we observe an art with a religious content produced by artists who are not identified with religious institutions; on the other hand we have the indifference of such institutions to members of their own faith, who, in a sincere way, undertook to produce works of a religious nature.

The explanations seem relatively clear. One is simply that churches are in one sense social institutions, and many artists tend to employ an idiom that is not socially acceptable. For hierarchy and laity alike – even today – the work of some contemporary artists can sometimes shock in relation to its sincerity. Second, one can partly account for this dissonance between religious institutions and religious art by noting a more general decline – itself a dimension of secularisation – in Europe at least, of the cultural role of the churches and in their relative failure to acknowledge and maintain what is new and fertile in the cultural and social life of the time. It has not always been so. In art-historical terms new styles of art were often if not always produced by artists who had developed those styles in tasks for the Church. Gothic architecture arose in the course of constructing churches. Similarly it was not primarily in secular art but in religious art (i.e. new programmes of church design and decoration) that Romanesque sculpture and Baroque painting arose, and the same may be said of stained glass. On the contrary, from the nineteenth century to the present, nearly all important developments in painting, sculpture and architecture have taken place largely outside the religious sphere, and their very existence was perceived as a challenge to the primacy of religion in spiritual, moral and social matters. Hence the Church had to ask to what extent would the adoption of these new styles of art, created in contexts so apparently foreign to the interests and mind-set of the Church, be a kind of counter-infection, a virus, introducing into religious thinking and feeling intrinsically secular conceptions which were regarded as incompatible with basic religious beliefs. This is the essential problem that has distinguished religious art, from the nineteenth to the twenty-first century, from both the rationale for, and the practice of, such art in previous centuries.

the aesthetic dimension

The aesthetic consequences of the institutional crisis outlined above are readily distinguishable and still with us. Most visible is what Tillich so caustically described as 'sentimental, beautifying naturalism ... the feeble drawing, the poverty of vision, the petty historicity of our church-sponsored art is not simply unendurable, but *incredible* ... it calls for iconoclasm.'[28] It will not suffer it, however. For one thing we continue to live at a time when the normative forms and images of the Judaeo-Christian tradition are still accessible to many at the level of nostalgia, if not necessarily as a living presence in their lives. Within the Protestant tradition, Holman Hunt's 'Light of the World', for example, rapidly became, in reproductions of varied price and quality, a widely distributed icon in many Victorian households, of whatever social class. Indeed, to judge from visitor comments and postcard sales at the London National Gallery exhibition 'Seeing Salvation' in 2000, it continues to occupy – along with Dalí's 'Christ of St John of the Cross' – a secure, if not necessarily revered, place in the religious psyches of many supposedly modern, secular, men and women. Similarly, in the United States, as David Morgan[29] and his colleagues have shown, Warner Sallman's 'Head of Christ' (1940) occupied an equally salient, and even more commercially successful, position as a – indeed *the* – central icon within the visual culture of American Protestantism, both conservative and liberal. For another reason, and especially, if not exclusively, within Roman Catholicism, religious art, whatever its aesthetic quality, carries its own crude inner logic. Such art is art useful to the Church, and art useful to the Church must be unambiguously catechetical. This is the lightly Platonised aesthetic which lies behind both the vulgar and banal pictures of Christ and Mary now in global circulation, and cheap, mass-produced icons of both which pervade Italy, Spain, and Central and South America. Sometimes such images have a dual function, in serving as vehicles for national identity as well as personal devotion. Mexico's 'Our Lady of Guadalupe' and Peru's 'Lord of the Miracles'[30] are perhaps the best-known examples of where aesthetic traditionalism works, paradoxically, to symbolise modern nationhood. In the Russian

Orthodox tradition, too, the famous 'Virgin of Vladimir', although Byzantine in origin, has long been, in Richard Temple's words, 'the chief *palladium* of the Russian state, protecting the Russian people, delivering them from enemies and performing many miracles'.[31] Even today Soviet newspapers and television news sometimes carry pictures of young conscripts en route for Chechnya filing past, and kissing, a replica of the 'Vladimir' icon proffered by an Orthodox priest.

Yet the alternative, for many contemporary artists, usually involves deliberately sidestepping any literal depiction of the Gospel because the prevailing, indeed dominant aesthetic is usually too narrow to permit it – proceeding, as it does, away from all literary content towards the 'universal' art of abstraction. Such abstraction, so long as it remains the dominant cultural mode, will continue to present to most religious institutions an art largely without symbols or imagery (and with any ambiguities 'de-symbolised' out of it) and therefore without any specific doctrinal allusion. At the same time, for many lay consumers, as Harold Rosenberg and others have argued, much of *all* abstract art remains psychologically inaccessible to secular Man, not only because he continues to think of art as primarily representation or ornament, but also because, as Rosenberg puts it

> the central language of modern art has already entered his consciousness indirectly, by way of the popular arts – advertising, TV, etc. But since the process *is* indirect, and quite detached from those orders of society to which he may already feel overtly committed – religion, politics, class formations, for example – the great images of modern art are never available for his inner nourishment.[32]

Such an argument may provide a powerful and pessimistic counterpoint both to facile aesthetic progressivism (not unknown, for example, in some contemporary clerical circles) and to the fashionable Jungian heresy (held by some theologians and artists alike) that 'the archetypes by which spiritual realities express themselves are both available to modern man and constantly clothed in the forms of modern art'.

Yet there is one way in which contemporary abstraction in art also carries with it some genuine credal resonance. It is one to which Hans Kung repeatedly draws our attention in his *Art and the Question of Meaning*. 'What', he asks, 'if in the course of modern development the idea of a pre-existing divine order of meaning has been increasingly shattered and this meaning itself has become more questionable?' Can the work of art still be meaningful when the great synthesis of meaning no longer exists? Kung's answer is that 'in a time of meaninglessness, the work of art can symbolise *meaninglessness* very precisely in a way that is aesthetically completely meaningful – that is to say, inwardly harmonious – and does so to a large extent in modern art'.[33] If he is right, then the most appropriate role model for today's artists (and one maybe to be encouraged by today's art teachers and theologians) is not necessarily to profess a specifically confessional commitment, nor to try to lift the current aesthetic taboo against explicit narrative content. It is rather to profess a self-guided religious imagination which no longer merely reflects existing religious tradition, but creates and expresses new spiritual perceptions which we are all invited to share. It was Paul Gauguin who urged that 'painting should return to its original purpose, the examination of the interior life of human beings'.[34] It was his near contemporary, the German sociologist Max Weber, who maintained that it is 'the profoundest aesthetic experience that provides an answer to one's seeking self'.[35]

This first chapter, which introduced four dimensions for understanding the relationship between seeing and believing – the iconographic, the didactic, the institutional and the aesthetic – is necessarily highly schematic. Although it contains a certain amount of supporting art-historical detail, it does not really attempt – except when discussing the Baroque – to depict the dynamic interplay of these dimensions within any specific cultural and credal context. The next three chapters are case studies which attempt to do precisely this.

2

art, religion and the victorians

If the 'religion' (defined by Durkheim as 'a system of beliefs and practices relative to sacred things') of the Victorians was often highly complex – nucleated not only around Christian beliefs and practices, but also around Progress, Work, Duty and other secular residues of the Protestant ethic, the precise role and status of their religious art were themselves distinctly paradoxical. At one level such art was thoroughly institutionalised at the top of a formal hierarchy acknowledged by painters, critics and public alike. The scale ran from 'popular' to 'High' art, or more precisely, from 'scenes domestic' through 'portraits', 'landscapes', 'subjects poetical and imaginative' to 'High Art, sacred and secular'. How would you define High Art?' the painter William Etty was asked by the Select Committee on Art Unions in 1845. He did so as 'History, Poetical subjects and such a class of landscapes as Poussin and others have painted … with scriptural subjects the highest of all.'[1] The high cultural status of the last was virtually unchallenged at the time. One reason was that there was strong consensus as to what the functions of such art should be. It should serve essentially 'religious' ends, reinforcing and echoing belief, appealing, in Etty's words, 'to those deep, mysterious and inward feelings of our nature which all must own, but no-one can define'. Sometimes it was presumed to have a more overtly didactic role. 'As the taste of the people proceeds to develop itself in art', Etty was asked by the same committee, 'might it not be desirable to make that increase in taste an instrument for increasing their devotional feeling … in fact form a new inlet for devotion?' Etty agreed. Sometimes such didacticism was tinged with unashamed expectations of behaviour modification. For example, in 1845 the Dean of Norwich proposed the introduction of 'scriptural subjects' into the annual exhibition of that city's Drawing Society so that 'our lower orders will be improved in a very short time'.[2]

Yet, although religious subject matter therefore enjoyed high formal status within the official canon of Victorian painting, and its didactic functions were freely acknowledged in Christian circles, its de facto position was, like so much of Victorian religion itself, far more marginal and uncertain. One reason for this was that within the overall canon of High Art, religious art tended in practice, as opposed to theory, to lack the superior status formally assigned to it. One indicator of this was the gradual but evident subordination of religious to secular historical themes as the most appropriate subject matter for High Art in public places – most notably in the decorative scheme for the new Houses of Parliament.[3] At the same time – in marked contrast to the Gothic or the Baroque, for example – the very specificity with which Victorian religious art's terms of reference were popularly spelt out also, paradoxically, reinforced its marginality and made it increasingly difficult for it to realise the pastoral and moral objectives formally assigned to it. Observe the well-known genre painter Frith reporting the following exchange at a Royal Academy exhibition in the late 1840s.

> An artist who seldom paints anything but what are called religious subjects saw some ladies eagerly scanning his work, when a gentleman came up to them and said 'What's that? Oh, a scripture piece. Don't waste time on that – it's very bad – all the scripture pieces are shocking this year.'[4]

This hiving off of religious subject matter to an increasingly specific place in the genre was, one might argue, both similar to and part of a broader secularising process which was already operating to relocate worship, theology, even belief itself, to a more discrete and implicitly marginal place in Victorian culture.

In purely economic terms, too, contemporary sales figures indicate that, prior to mid-century, there was little or no market, and certainly no popular demand, for *all* High Art whether sacred or secular. As for religious art itself, three specific constraints operated. One was the lack of patronage by the Established Church. Indeed it was ironical, if perhaps inevitable, that the massive church-building or 'extension' programme from 1830 to 1850 had so little aesthetic spin-off as far as the visual arts were concerned. Official Church policy is exemplified in the Anglican grandee Lord Bexley's remark to the painter Benjamin Haydon, 'Let us build churches first, Mr Haydon, and think of decorating them afterwards.'[5] But the constraints were not merely utilitarian. They were also ideological. Indeed their source lay with the Reformation itself. As the critic Samuel Redgrave put it, 'Protestant Britain has never quite overcome the objections of her Reformers to Scriptural subjects.'[6]

This 'Protestant yoke' argument was frequently invoked throughout the 1830s and 1840s. Beneath it, of course, was the association – at both elite and popular levels – of religious painting with 'Romanism'. Elite attitudes were profoundly shaped by those of the leading critic John Ruskin, who, for example, did not hesitate to describe a relatively innocuous genre picture by Collins called 'Convent Thoughts' (now in the Ashmolean Museum, Oxford, it depicts a novice daydreaming of her pre-convent days) to his readers as 'Romanizing and Tractarian'.[7] Ruskin's influence reached deep down into the religious art market. The Pre-Raphaelite Dante Gabriel Rossetti told his brother how he touched up a painting of his for sale to a wealthy ship-owner. 'It has now lost it's familiar name of the "Ancilla". It is now "the Annunciation". The mottoes have now been altered from Latin to English to guard against the imputation of Popery.'[8] Hedged about by such constraints, it is unsurprising therefore that Victorian paintings of religious themes, although possessing, as we have seen, an explicit if diminishing role and status, also had no really significant market.

Until the mid-nineteenth century, that is. For what seems very clear is that between the 1850s and 1880s, just when two

Religious subjects exhibited and purchased at the Royal Academy, in relation to total number of exhibits

	(a) *exibited*	(b) *purchased*
1841	6 out of 381	3 out of 6
1851	9 out of 399	8 out of 9
1861	16 out of 403	16 out of 16
1871	22 out of 401	20 out of 22
1881	28 out of 407	26 out of 28

of the most customarily invoked pointers towards secularisation – falling practice and increasing religious doubt – were attaining visible momentum, there was an equally visible boom in the religious art market. Indeed if one analyses those paintings of religious subject matter (a) exhibited, and (b) purchased at the annual Royal Academy Exhibitions between 1841 and 1881,[9] the figures speak for themselves.

Such a boom is fairly dramatic in percentage terms. Indeed its overall trajectory may even mirror – culturally if not statistically – the complex and still problematic chronology of the so-called Victorian 'crisis of faith' itself. This awaits more detailed investigation.[10]

What kind of explanations are we to seek for such an apparently inverse relationship between religious art and religious belief – between seeing and believing? There are plenty available. An art-historical one would include the critical role of Pre-Raphaelitism and the Oxford Movement in heightening the aesthetic and religious sensibilities of a whole cohort of younger patrons whose fathers, in the 1830s and 1840s, had been deeply antagonised by the same phenomena. Architectural historians would probably opt for the increasing dominance, largely induced by Butterfield and Pugin, of a historicist, neo-Gothic conception of 'total' church architecture, incorporating altarpieces and murals as near-mandatory components of their decorative schemes. Economic and cultural historians might point more towards the impact of increasing religious toleration and diminishing anti-Catholicism upon the production, distribution and consumption of religious artefacts. Indeed, while the relationship between religious conflict and religious art is always a highly complex one, in the Victorian era it is almost as if the market for religious art rose as religious tolerance itself increased.

Yet while such differing interpretations clearly carry some force, four more overtly sociological explanations also suggest themselves. The first is the strong evidence for a change in the patronage base for religious art towards what one contemporary described as 'the multiplication of middling fortunes in this country'. Yet the social composition per se of the major patron group is not of paramount importance here. The key question is rather, 'what do those who patronized religious art in any significant way at this time have in common?' First, such patronage is provincial rather than metropolitan – notably Tyneside, Birmingham, the West Riding and Liverpool/Birkenhead – all urban centres possessing strong traditions of provincial particularism, flourishing Mechanics' Institutes and Art Unions, and a well-developed local cultural life. In such a context the purchase of religious art to decorate the new public buildings in such centres (Leeds and Manchester Town Halls are the most famous examples) was one of the ways in which an upwardly mobile local elite could (not unlike their earlier equivalents in Siena or Bruges) express their secular social status. To judge from the primary sources, their fundamental impulse was less religious than paternalistic and philanthropic – a kind of aesthetic analogue to the similar attitudes already deployed by such men towards their own workforces.

More significantly, the overwhelming proportion of those who purchased religious art *for themselves* at this time, thereby contributing to the sales boom documented above, were religious Nonconformists of one hue or another. Clearly this is not the whole picture. There were major mid-Victorian purchasers of religious art who were neither provincial nor Nonconformist. Prince Albert is, of course, the best known. Nor is there any suggestion that even the most pious Nonconformist collectors opted for religious subject matter only, or that their motives for so doing were always or overtly religious. Consider one such patron – Gibbons, a West Midlands iron-master, and Congregationalist, talking of a recent purchase at the 1844 Royal Academy.

> Boxall's little thing is altogether ideal. It is a personification of Hope, or Faith or some religious sentiment or other, and therefore one does not look for nature (in the common sense of the word) in it. If it has an abstract beauty it is enough. I am not fond of this class of pictures but variety is good in a collection and one or two of them it is as well to have.[11]

At one level, such activity – like commissioning a villa in the latest taste – was simply one way in which newly acquired social status was visually articulated. At another it may also symbolise the initiatives – political, social and educational – which rising Nonconformist elites were now seizing from their Anglican neighbours. In this sense such patronage of religious art was highly functional. There are also hints, from certain primary sources, that such paintings may have served, especially for some Nonconformist patrons (in a fashion analogous to the sexual double standard portrayed by Steven Marcus in *The Other Victorians*[12]), as a private, potent and culturally approved set of aesthetic and religious sensations which the sobriety and sensory deprivation of chapel culture officially denied them. Here, not for the first time in the history of art, religious art may have helped certain individuals (to adapt Bernstein's terminology[13]) to articulate a kind of 'extended code' of private religiosity which compensated for the 'restricted code' usually to be found within Protestant Dissent.

The second explanation is more explicitly technological. It concerns the popularising of Victorian religious art through a revolution in engraving techniques. This rapidly disseminated and democratised, in reproduction form, all kinds of art, especially 'High' art. There was a lush subculture of such material. Some were simply serial art magazines which kept a constant flow of religious pictures – classical and contemporary – before the reading public. Even more relevant for this discussion is the growth of quasi-literary, quasi-devotional, quasi-aesthetic magazines like *Good Words* and *Sunday at Home*.[14] Indeed, the latter title is itself an excellent indicator of a Victorian Sabbath in which worship itself now had a diminishing salience. The Pre-Raphaelites were well-established contributors to such publications. A third stream, well-developed by the 1880s, was a flood of books with titles like *From Bethlehem to Olivet – Pictures by Modern Painters of the Life of Christ*. These, and others like them – religious coffee-table books for the middle-class market – marked a new and significant departure from the days when even a vellum binding might well excite suspicions of Popery. In addition, led by Ernest Gambart,[15] a highly entrepreneurial dealer, the entire engravings industry became increasingly professionalised. Gambart, for example, bought Holman Hunt's 'Light of the World' (*Figure 5*) with copyright for £5,500, and at his death in 1902 well over three-quarters of a million reproductions of the painting had been produced and distributed. The figures are not in fact outstanding by late Victorian standards. But what is crucial – especially in the light of assumptions about the growth in these years of a popular 'culture of unbelief', is the creation – possibly for the first time, and certainly since the Reformation – of a cheap, accessible and above all genuinely Protestant iconography. Indeed such a painting as 'The Light of the World' took on a quite explicitly votive function in working-class as well as middle-class homes – just what Englishmen often criticised Popery itself for doing, with its images of the Virgin among Catholics in Ireland and elsewhere.

However coarse the aesthetic consequences, the cultural consequences of such technical change was in effect to help transfer the locus of mid-Victorian religious art away from the realm of High Art to that of popular culture. And this just at the time when some observers were openly lamenting the passage of formalised religious beliefs and practice *away* from popular culture and towards a middle- and upper-class minority!

This brings us to a third explanation for such an apparent boom in mid-Victorian religious art. It is that if one looks at what religious subjects were painted, by whom, and to what cultural specifications, two identifiable mutations in subject matter seem to have taken place. One is that with its relocation from High Art to popular culture, the religious theme, instead of remaining a subspecies of High Art (accorded, as we have seen, the highest formal status) becomes more consciously subsumed under the 'narrative' genre (what the Academy would have classified earlier as 'Division 5 – Scenes Domestic'). Yet, although this transition is to some extent paralleled by the rise of the 'three-decker' novel as a characteristically mid-nineteenth-century art form, it is not altogether clear why *religious* painting – especially at a time of heightened secular challenges in other religious spheres – should swing so sharply in this direction. One reason might be the growth of a more 'secular' historiography – spearheaded by Macaulay and Hallam – which increasingly led to a demand for a similarly objective, demystified version of 'sacred' history. Another might be that the spread of relatively cheap reproductions, through the Arundel Society and others, made the more affluent members of a print-buying middle class more aware, for the first time, of the narrative cycles in medieval and early Renaissance painting. Either way, in the second half of the nineteenth century, religious painting became essentially part of literary or narrative painting. In practice the transformation of the genre took three distinct, if often interlocking, forms.

One is that religious paintings come to bear increasingly lengthy titles and increasingly cumbrous accompanying notes supplied by the artist. Second, certain traditional themes – notably the Holy Family – were painted and merchandised with a more overt emphasis upon their contemporary, secular and domestic relevance. Here, for example, is Armitage, a highly successful painter of religious subjects, lecturing to Royal Academy students in the 1860s on the Holy Family as subject matter.

> I should think there are at least a thousand original Holy Families in existence: and yet the subject seems as fresh to me as ever. The reason is that the subject embodies the purest form of human love, and echoes the religion of the home, the ideal of family life in our own time.[16]

The contrast here to the lofty spiritual purposes of High Art forty years earlier is self-evident. This reworking of an orthodox theme in Christian narrative to serve contemporary, secular, didactic ends is not only fascinating in itself, but goes some way towards explaining how the boom in religious art was not wholly incompatible with a weakening of both belief and practice over the same period. Such religious art as this not only fused with but reaffirmed secular bourgeois morality.

The third adaptation of the religious genre is a reversal of this process – a kind of inverted secularism. Here, instead of religious art being directed in style and content towards its secular analogues, contemporary, secular and usually domestic subject matter was itself invested with a fairly explicit religious coda. As the *P.R.B. Journal* put it: 'If our best and most original ideas come from our own times, why transfer them to distant periods? Why teach us to revere the saints of old and not our own family worshippers? Why worship a martyred St Agatha and not a sick woman?'[17] This conscious dismantling of the formal barriers between the sacred and the secular as legitimate subject matter for a 'religious' painting – even if it was to degenerate ultimately into artworks which did little more than either portray a covertly religious theme in an overtly religious setting ('Contemplation' was a typical title) or depict religious activity per se ('Her First Sermon' or 'Late for Church') while making no credal statement whatever – was a clear indicator of the relatively uncertain passage of the process of secularisation already manifesting itself in this particular culture.

The fourth and final mid-Victorian adaptation of subject matter within the religious genre served equally explicit ends. This was the replacing of the evidently mythic by an explicit naturalism, reinforced, where possible, by historical verisimilitude. Such a commitment to authenticity, both in feeling and expression, had its roots, of course, deep in early-nineteenth-century romanticism. Yet it seems clear – not least from the sales figures – that what Ruskin described as 'the sternly materialistic though deeply reverent veracity with which alone of all schools of painters the Brotherhood of Englishmen has conceived the life of Christ'[18] was precisely what High Victorian Protestantism required. The salient features of that Protestantism – the right of private judgement (i.e. accountable to God alone) and reverence for the Bible itself rendered both veracity and naturalism imperative. Even the most unreconstructed fundamentalists could make an aesthetic as well as a credal response to what W.M. Rossetti called 'conscientious scriptural history representations in which the aim is to adhere strictly to the recorded fact, merely transferring it from verbal expression to form ... the fidelity of the transfer will be the arbiter appealed to'.[19] Public demands for such veracity not only led to some very laboured paintings (Britain's provincial art galleries contain many examples), but to a preoccupation, in both Old and New Testament subject matter, with topographical realism and sartorial exactitude that sometimes bordered on the obsessive. Indeed it could well be argued that as the literal interpretation of Scripture became increasingly questioned, and the historical Jesus partly demythologised (especially by German scholarship), so painters of religious themes sought − at times quite consciously − to sustain Christian morale by underlining the visual authenticity of the settings for Bible narrative, even if the literal truth of the narrative itself was being increasingly treated with scholarly scepticism. They also sold more paintings that way.

This case study has necessarily focused upon religious art in a specific cultural and historical context. It has sought explanations for the persistence, indeed growth, of this art in such factors as changes in the patronage base, the democratisation of religious themes through their relocation within popular culture, and the adaptation of the content of the genre itself to meet new needs and expectations. To these might be added

– far more tentatively – what could be described as a stylistic transformation within Victorian religious art itself. A preliminary analysis of the titles of pictures submitted to the Royal Academy between 1841 and 1881 suggests an apparent shift in the subject matter of religious paintings away from comparatively static themes (presented as a kind of 'still' from a cinematic Bible) towards relatively dramatic subjects (notably the Passion and the Transfiguration). Subsequent scrutiny of the paintings themselves (or reproductions of them) clearly reveals a marked stylistic transition over the same period, between the kind of low-definition pietism (found in Rossetti's 'Girlhood of Mary Virgin', for example) of the 1840s towards the high-definition mannerism of the 1870s and 1880s (for example, Edwin Long or G.F. Watts) where the composition is more dramatic, the chiaroscuro heavily accented and the physical proportions more often attenuated. Superficially such a stylistic transition – from pietism to mannerism[20] – strongly parallels what had already happened in Italian religious art between Duccio and Caravaggio, or in French sacred music between Cherubini and Berlioz. Without pressing the point too far, all three stylistic transformations, if culturally distinct, also occurred precisely when extensive and comparatively rapid changes – rooted in industrialisation, humanism and revolutionary romanticism respectively – were taking place outside and within religion itself.

In sum, although the choice of Victorian religious art may seem an unduly narrow and aesthetically unrewarding one, and some of the supporting detail wholly unfamiliar to non-specialists, it also underlines the extremely complicated matrix of beliefs and practices, values and motives, patron, artist and public that underpins *all* religious art. Three broader conclusions can also be drawn. One is that whenever or whatever secularising processes manifest themselves historically, the relationship of religious art to such processes is neither constant, nor convergent nor divergent. Nor is the historical evidence for a supposedly widening gap appearing between religiousness and religious art (from Early Christian catacomb painting to the Vence Chapel, as it were) as societies themselves become more complex or advanced quite as conclusive as might be presumed. In nineteenth-century Britain at least, as we have seen, the 'gap' widens, and then narrows again, irrespective of transformations in belief and practice. Second, when a radical change occurs in a culture it does not necessarily, as the social anthropologist Sir Raymond Firth maintained, 'destroy the *raison d'être* of a particular form of art'. Indeed within Victorian religion and art the reverse seems to have been the case. Elite demand for religious art objects actually rose, and a popular iconography flourished, just when traditional beliefs were being eroded and formal religious practice was in apparent decline. In this sense the locus of religiosity seems to have partly shifted from the credal and ritual to the physically symbolic mode.

Finally, in relating the aesthetic sphere to religion, not only, as Max Weber had noted in 1910, had the various arts served religious and magical purposes, but also 'under the development of intellectualism and the rationalization of life ... art becomes a cosmos of more and more consciously grasped independent values which exist in their own right'.[21] Indeed, as a distinct institution, he argues, 'art takes over the function of a this-worldly salvation', competing directly with religion and transforming 'judgements of moral intent into judgements of taste'. Art thus competes with religion as another set of supreme values antithetical to those prevailing in society. These values, he suggests, include 'salvation' from the routines of everyday life and from the 'pressures of theoretical and practical realism'. Yet, at least on the evidence we have drawn from this Victorian case study, art, far from competing with religion in the fashion adduced by Weber, itself became a symbolically powerful and pervasive repository for religious values. As such, religious art itself, especially after 1850, seemed to enjoy almost autonomous occupation of the mid-ground between the 'religious' and the 'secular'.

3

seeing salvation

Our second case study is concerned less with the place of religious art in a particular time frame and more with the impact of such art upon the individual viewer. Again the issue is a highly complicated one, especially within contemporary culture. For one thing, comparatively little is known, not least empirically, about the responses of believers and unbelievers alike to religious subject matter, whether in church, temple or gallery.[1] What kind of 'transaction' does take place, and can we ever pinpoint the interstices of 'religious' and 'aesthetic' experience, or discover how deep-laid, personal and complex such a process is? Occasionally a random act of desecration by a disturbed individual makes global headlines, but the character and content of personal responses to, for example, the sculptural programme of the Royal Portal at Chartres, or the Rubens 'Adoration' in King's College Chapel in Cambridge, or the Sistine Chapel – let alone the religious subject matter routinely displayed in national and provincial galleries – remain tantalisingly undocumented. Even museums explicitly devoted to such art – in Utrecht, New York and Glasgow, for example – do not seem to have had the time, resources or perhaps the inclination to secure any systematic feedback from their visitors.

There are, in any case, some very powerful cultural constraints already at work. One is perhaps the declining power and efficacy of traditional Christian symbolism. At its most mundane the process involves the wilful appropriation of sacred symbols by secular institutions, notably the advertising industry and the media, and their apparent desacralisation to serve material rather than spiritual ends. For example, for many, the footballer David Beckham currently enjoys iconic parity, worldwide, with Jesus Christ, as did the singer Madonna with *the* Madonna less than a decade ago. At a deeper level the central question is whether or not the spiritual voltage of orthodox Christian symbolism is now so reduced that such symbols can no longer function to bind people to each other within a common relatedness to God through Christ. Put differently, are the major Christian symbols still able to stir the imagination and convey vision and prophecy, or must they be abandoned in favour of others? And, if not abandoned, must they be drastically reconceived and reformulated in order that they may become a real power within post-Christian society, serving to relate human experience to ultimate mystery? Or is it already too late, and for many Christian iconography is already experienced primarily as a dead language – like Sanskrit or ancient Egyptian hieroglyphics – rather than as part of a living faith.

A second difficulty is an equally explicit one. It is simply that it is far easier to attribute a spiritual dimension to art objects than to discern the precise spiritual properties that these objects hold for individuals. If the latter *were* possible, and very few psychologists are, alas, interested in attempting it, then a Nobel Prize for Religious Aesthetics would be there for the taking. But history, too, is not on our side. Whereas the Abbot Suger could speak of a St Denis where God was worshipped most highly in attributes of light, measure and number, it may be far more difficult nowadays for individuals to identify, let alone experience, the spiritual in a postmodern culture where religious consciousness – indeed all consciousness – is so fractured and diffuse. One consequence of this is the striking contemporary paradox of a highly visual culture in which Christian imagery per se has itself become increasingly invisible.

A third constraint on a creative and meaningful interplay between art and religions may be – another paradox here – the critical role of the modern museum in what might be called the desacralisation of religious art itself. The process is not wholly a contemporary one. T.S. Eliot's acid description in the 'Love Song of J. Alfred Prufrock' of how 'In the room, the women come and go/ Talking of Michelangelo' was, after all, written in 1917. But as Andrée Hayum, taking her cue from Walter Benjamin, has written, 'As the movable picture entered the museum, earlier examples – religious art in particular – were stripped of their former affective power … and aesthetic veneration could supplant religious devotion.'[2] Her argument is suggestive, if not wholly persuasive, because it is difficult to see precisely *why* such paintings should be shorn of their 'religious' qualities simply because they are no longer in an ecclesiastical setting. Again, research is needed. Unfortunately Professor Peter Abbs's current empirical work on aesthetic experience pays no specific attention to religious artefacts, while the brilliant 'Art of Devotion' exhibition at the Rijksmuseum in 1995, with its conscious strategy of enforcing, in a deliberately darkened gallery, individual attention upon single, spotlit devotional objects from the High Middle Ages, also failed to carry out any systematic analysis of visitor responses.

However, in 2000 a major opportunity presented itself. In that year, as part of the millennial celebrations, the National Gallery staged a major exhibition titled 'Seeing Salvation – the Image of Christ'.[3] It aimed to show how the figure of Christ has been represented in the Western tradition, and to explore the power of the religious image within that tradition. It also sought, as the catalogue put it, 'to demonstrate that modern secular audiences can engage with the masterpieces of Christian art at an emotional as well as a purely aesthetic or historical level'. The exhibition was phenomenally successful, averaging over five thousand visitors per day over four and a half months, and breaking box-office records for any British art exhibition of the previous two decades. It is unsurprising, therefore, that as a sociologist with an interest in religion and aesthetics I should want to explore the apparent paradox of the success of such an exhibition in a society recently described by the French academic René Rémond as 'one of the most secular in Europe'[4] by paying particular attention to the motives, expectations and experiences of those who visited it. To do so, I drew upon four sources of information – interviews with individuals immediately after they had seen the exhibition; the findings of a market-research inquiry – commissioned by the Gallery – into visitor responses to the exhibition itself and accompanying public lectures and television programmes; interviews, carried out by a graduate student of mine, with most of the major art critics who covered the show; finally, and most fruitfully, the three hundred or so letters of appreciation and denigration sent to the Gallery's director by individuals subsequent to their visit. From these four sources I was able to identify two distinct, yet often interconnected, patterns of public response to such an exhibition, which I will describe as the 'transactional' and the 'experiential'. The former reflect some, if not all, of the four dimensions of the relationship between religious art and religious belief – iconographic, didactic, institutional and aesthetic – set out in the opening chapter. The latter press even closer to the personal experience of individuals. Both emerge from the written and oral testimonies of those visitors to 'Seeing Salvation' whose own voices can be so clearly heard throughout what follows.

transactions

Four differing kinds were readily identifiable. The first can be described as *cognitive*. For example, 'I knew that I was somewhere special', or 'it was a most enlightening and moving experience', or, again, 'I had seen "Seeing Salvation" as heritage, albeit a shared religious heritage, rather than a locus of vital religious experience.' Finally, and more explicitly, 'the space was jammed with people, but all with such a sense of the contemplative, allowing the works gathered to speak in many diverse ways to those before them.'

The second kind of perceived transaction was more overtly *didactic*, where visitors often saw the exhibition as essentially a learning experience, and one where they could readily link form to function in religious art. For example, 'I realised that this was part of my religious heritage. Indeed it took me back to my schooldays', or 'I learned a lot … it gave me new insights.… I found myself focusing on meaning rather than composition, line, colour, form or tone', and even more explicitly, 'Here were well-loved paintings presented in a new light as aids to devotion besides being great works of art. Hidden meanings, often lost to the modern viewer are revealed to increase understanding.' Others, however, perceived such didacticism quite differently. 'I objected', wrote one, 'very much to some of the captions in the exhibition. By using phrases like "Our Lord" and "Jesus Our Saviour" the National Gallery was surely proselytising for a particular religion while claiming that it was not.' Other reactions were more subtle.

> The paintings do not really belong in Trafalgar Square anyway: at some time in the past they were removed from churches and other places where they had a clearly devotional purpose. But there they are still unmistakably devoted to that purpose, though it is a purpose no longer clearly understood. More of us look at them with some quite different, ill-defined, but un-devotional motive.

The third type of personal transaction evidenced by visitor responses is best described as *iconographic*, in that it attests to the power of images per se. 'These are images that teach the Faith', asserted one viewer firmly, while another reflected, far less unequivocally, that although 'I am not a practising Christian, I was moved to tears by many of the images'. A third remained convinced that 'Images of Christ – in Passion, Sorrow, on the Cross – are ingrained on our minds. Like it or not these epic images seep in and touch us in a peculiarly penetrating way.' Listen, too, to a more overtly secular appraisal of religious images as part of essentially aesthetic experience. 'There were only a very few of the items that I found inspirational. But it was a privilege to view these wonderful things free of charge, and thank God [*sic*] there are still a few oases of wonder left in this country.' For others it was an opportunity to articulate a more overtly agnostic stance on the historical veracity of the Christ image ('how do we know he had a beard?') or to comment, very acutely, that 'although Christian iconography is a vocabulary or language with which we are now unfamiliar, the central question is how have we formed this image, and how has this image formed us over two thousand years?' – a question indeed at the heart of this study.

Interestingly the 'Seeing Salvation' research encountered two very striking instances of where Christian imagery had been specifically appropriated and applied to personal circumstances. One was at a public lecture (given by one of the exhibition's curators, and attended by the author) where a female member of the audience shyly stood up and confessed that she had just undergone a 'religious' experience, activated by an early-fifteenth-century miniature crib in which the infant Jesus lay stiff in a posture reminiscent of the cot death of one of her own children. Yet, while in the public discussion that followed the lecture many of the audience described the specific exhibit as 'emotionally powerful', 'affecting', and so forth, only one, the woman already cited, chose to describe her own gallery experience as 'religious'. The second example is more poignant still. Consider here another viewer, writing to the director, from a fashionable London address, ostensibly asking him to sign her copy of the catalogue. In the last paragraph she writes

> Please accept my praises, which are sincere ... my son, my only child, died of anorexia two and a half years ago at the age of 26.... I found the exhibition intensely moving and as a mother who has just lost her son (Jamie was eight weeks on the life support and I watched him dying inch by inch, day by day) unforgettable in its imagery and emotion. Thank you.

The final type of transaction suggested by the data gathered is less psychologically complex than the preceding three. It can perhaps best be described as *credal*, in the sense of seeing the exhibition as affirming and legitimating Christian belief and identity in general as well as a kind of personal Christology in particular. Here is one typical example, 'I'm one of those large numbers of people who perhaps feel that Christianity is unfashionable, neglected by the media and unacceptable as part of national cultural life. We were grateful for this exception to the rule.' Or another, who wrote to the director that 'It made for some of the most effective religious broadcasting that

I have seen', and a third who surmised, even more succinctly, 'Art drew people to God once – perhaps it could do so again?' Not everybody took this position. One of those interviewed remarked that although the exhibition clearly articulated such doctrines as the Incarnation and the Immaculate Conception, as far as he was concerned, 'I find what seems to be a require-ment to believe in these and other points of dogma an irksome imposition.' Another was even more robust: 'Frankly I found the show yawn-inducing.… "Seeing Salvation" makes you feel like Christianity itself needs a bit of saving.'

experiences

The four types of transaction outlined above are, of course presented – in the interests of clarity – in a deliberately over-schematic way. Indeed the same raw research materials not only yield (as we have seen) an identifiable set of transactions between viewers, exhibition subject, setting, and the art ob-jects themselves, but also point to a wide spectrum of richly variegated visitor experiences. At one end was what, following William James,[5] can best be described as the 'sense of presence' experience. Sometimes this was expressed in overtly theological language. For example, 'in an overwhelmingly secular age … it is still possible to pick up signals of transcendence – to gain a glimpse of the grace that is to be found on, with, and beneath the everyday reality of our lives'. More frequently, the language used was overtly personal and emotive.

> The exhibition drew one's mind with such depth of thought and feeling, quite inexpressible in words. And strangely, I felt other people were expressing something quite unique. There was an atmosphere which was almost tangible. Despite the queues and the heat there was no jostling and no noise. There was a quietness, a silence, a hush, as if the pictures and the artefacts exerted a powerful hold on the visitors.

Or again, 'the space was jammed with people, but all with a sense of the contemplative, allowing the works gathered to speak in many diverse ways to those before them. This was particularly special and very rare, to have a truly meaningful spiritual experience in a very crowded art gallery, I mean.' And finally, 'it was like going into a cathedral, and the atmosphere among the other people was quite astonishing – we were full of awe, sorrow and reverence. It was quite astonishing.'

Less intense, and hence further in along our spectrum from the 'sense of presence' experience, was what might be called 'the pilgrim presence'. Sometimes this was quite explicitly acknowledged, especially by those with professed religious affiliations, such as the Roman Catholic priest from Cardiff who recalled 'yes, "pilgrimage" was the slightly pompous title which we gave to our visit. It was pooh-poohed by some of my colleagues, but all who came felt that we had indeed had our faith deepened and our hope renewed', or the female churchgoer who wrote that 'it was wonderful ... wandering through the rooms became a pilgrimage following Christ's life'. Less predictable, but perhaps more arresting, were the reports from the ever-observant gallery attendants that 'we saw some people praying in front of images in the exhibition as they moved around' – a telling reaffirmation of the originally devotional character of many of the 'Seeing Salvation' exhibits.

A third point on the spectrum can be described as the 'loosely numinous', as when people reported that 'I felt we hadn't entirely left the spiritual in art behind', or that 'it gave me new insights and different emotional and spiritual responses'. It is perhaps worth noting here that the use of the word 'spiritual' in this context was almost exclusively confined to those whose responses to their visit fell squarely within the 'loosely numinous' category – in marked contrast to the current North American penchant (well documented by Wuthnow[6] and others) for using the same word to embrace all and any forms of personal religious experience! Close to the 'loosely numinous' on our spectrum was a similar, yet also differing, set of visitor responses. These can be described as 'secular historicist', in the same sense in which, as we have already seen in our first case study, earlier Victorian visitors to the National Gallery saw much religious painting as essentially mainstream 'history painting'. Hence one visitor could write to the director saying 'thank you for encouraging me to go into sections of the Gallery that I usually ignore, i.e. religion, and helping me to appreciate works of art that I usually walk past hurriedly to get to my favourite periods', while another could consciously invert this process by confessing 'I came to this exhibition as a Christian, but I now wish to visit the Gallery as an art lover (in training). Thank you.' A third, and more conventional, strand of historicism was that of those who were already aware of the connections between Christian art and the development of Western culture' and were only too happy to have this reinforced. 'Here on display', as one remarked, 'is the heart of the religion which nourished Western culture from the beginning.... this should help us to maintain a connection with our shared Christian heritage.'

Finally, there were those – a not insignificant quarter of respondents – situated at the opposite end of our experiential spectrum, whose reaction to their visit was 'essentially negative'. Some we've heard from already, such as those who feared proselytisation, those who had serious doubts about the historical veracity of Imago Christi ('how', asked one, 'could we come to decide what Christ looked like?') and those who felt that Christianity, even God, was now dead, or at least dying. A more widespread caveat was essentially sceptical, and profoundly aware of 'inhabiting a society, a secular society where religion has become irrelevant and has nothing valuable to offer, both in terms of its art and in terms of its moral principles'. At this extreme end of the spectrum, the 'Seeing Salvation' exhibition proved for one visitor 'an occasion where I saw everything but felt nothing'.

This case study has, necessarily, been heavily dependent on documentary evidence provided by visitors to an exceptionally successful exhibition of religious art. Some of the reasons for that success are relatively superficial – the fact that the exhibition was free, that it received very extensive and favourable media coverage, not only in the press but on television (where a series of four programmes were presented by the director,[7] an exceptional communicator, averaging a weekly audience of 700,000), and that it was very effectively promoted by and through the churches – yet also not insignificant. At a deeper level, the 'transactions' and 'experiences' reported in the research also point towards some other levels of explanation. One is that while many – visitors and art critics alike – saw 'Seeing Salvation' as heritage, albeit a shared *religious* heritage, rather than as a focus for primary religious experience, their reactions also demonstrate that modern secular audiences can engage with Christian art at an emotional as well as a purely aesthetic or historical level. Secondly, on this evidence, it is clear that in some circumstances religious art in an ostensibly secular setting such as the National Gallery can also serve as an effective vehicle for religious meaning.[8] Indeed in this sense 'Seeing Salvation' offered a powerful corrective to the conventional contention that museum culture effectively desacralises religious art. As the sociologist Roger Homan so eloquently put it in his own letter to the director,

> There is a sense in which galleries have plundered the pictured prayers of devout men, and students of art have lost interest in their subject matter. Hence I greatly welcome your recovery of the devotional intentions of artists and the focus upon their religious themes instead of their technical virtuosity.

One consequence may be that such exhibitions as this (the 2005 'Caravaggio – the Final Years', also at the National Gallery, is the most recent example) can still serve to articulate and sustain religious vocabulary in today's secular world. Indeed as one visitor to 'Seeing Salvation' commented, 'it was the first time – at least in our corner of the globe – that the theological content of works of Western art has been demonstrated with the same seriousness that is assumed for icons, etc., in the Orthodox East.'

From this, two conclusions might follow, One is that, on the evidence of this case study at least, it is clear that in an overwhelmingly secular age (in which the sheer plausibility of religious perceptions of reality seems to be weakening among large numbers of people) it is still possible to pick up signals of transcendence – to gain a glimpse of the grace that is to be found in, with and beneath the empirical reality of our lives. The other is, more prosaically, that in a predominantly post-Christian culture like our own, it seems that the relationship between religion and the visual arts, and especially between aesthetic and religious experience, is not necessarily as tenuous or problematic as it is so often presumed to be.

4

patron and artist

If the two case studies discussed so far have focused, quite deliberately, upon a specific cultural-historical context (Victorian Britain) and upon a specific exhibition ('Seeing Salvation'), the third pays close attention to the relationship between patron, artist and public in a specific, localised, setting. It is not one that has enjoyed a particularly high profile among art historians or within global tourism. It is not a response to monarchical, papal, episcopal or wealthy lay patronage. It is no Saint-Chapelle, or Sistine or Scrovegni Chapel, nor is it Matisse at Vence, or Rothko in Houston or even Spencer at Sandham. These sites, and many others, have all received meticulous and sustained scholarly attention. St Matthew's, Northampton, has not, although the story to be told, and the highly complex matrix of relationships involved – between theology, the art market, artworks and built form; congregation, donor, artist and public – is exceptionally revealing.

St Matthew's[1] is not an ancient church. Indeed from the outside it looks very like many other Victorian churches designed in the Gothic style and erected in the late nineteenth century to serve a new suburb of a rapidly growing provincial town. It was built (as local residents never tire of telling one) from the profits of beer, in that it was paid for by the family of a rich local brewer, Pickering Phipps, who, like so many successful Victorian businessmen, felt (I quote) that 'we Phipps must give back to the God who has blessed us with prosperity' – sentiments that would have been wholly intelligible to a Medici or a Flemish wool magnate. Externally St Matthew's is a very triumphalist structure. With a 170-foot tower and spire and an elaborate, richly ornamented *flèche* over the crossing, it was intended to signify a strong High Church presence at a time when Northampton had an atheist MP, Charles Bradlaugh, and a predominantly Nonconformist political elite. Today its triumphalism is relatively muted, and its urban setting now relatively unprepossessing.

Consecrated in 1893, St Matthew's had as its first incumbent Rowden Hussey, a high churchman from a wealthy Wiltshire farming family, who was to marry an equally wealthy Northamptonshire farmer's daughter and remain at St Matthew's for forty-eight years. His younger son, John Walter Hussey,[2] was born in 1909, and it is he who is integral to this case study. The biographical facts are simply recited. Son and grandson of a priest; schooling at Marlborough; PPE at Keble College, Oxford; Cuddesdon Theological College; curate at St Mary Abbott, Kensington; and priest-in-charge at St Paul's, Knightsbridge; then back, largely through filial compulsion, to his father's church in Northampton in 1936, where he was incumbent for the next eighteen years, before becoming Dean of Chichester in 1955. He remained unmarried and died in 1985. In one sense Hussey's is a very Anglican career trajectory, with two significant variants. He was always comfortably off, if never seriously rich. He was also passionately interested in the Arts – especially music, painting and sculpture. Indeed his – it must be said – rather unrevealing personal memoir recalls how, as a young priest in Knightsbridge, he went frequently to concerts and to the opera, and also 'managed to find time' to trawl London's commercial galleries and auction houses, and to begin to build up a private collection of his own. His tastes were essentially modern and occasionally avant-garde.

What is also highly significant here is not that Hussey was clearly, on this evidence, a well-heeled clerical aesthete, but that he was already also equally committed to what he was later to call 'art in the service of God'. 'I was aware', he recalled, 'that in years past the Church had so often commissioned music and painting and sculpture and I felt I had a great longing to do the same.'[3] The musical fulfilment of that longing does not strictly concern us here, but the visual consequences of it are central to this case study.

In 1942 Hussey had seen an exhibition of pictures by war artists – artists who had been commissioned by government to record various aspects life in the armed forces or in wartime civilian life. 'I was tremendously impressed by drawings of people sheltering in the underground during air raids', Hussey recalled,

the drawings had been made by Henry Moore, an artist of
whom I had not heard at the time, nor indeed had many people.
When I returned to Northampton … I told Harold Williamson
[Principal of the Chelsea College of Art then evacuated to
Northampton] how impressed I had been by Moore's drawings,
their dignity and three-dimensional quality seemed to make
anything that was unfortunate enough to be hanging near them
appear flat and dull. Warming to the subject I remember shaking
my finger at him and saying, 'That is the sort of man who ought
to be working for the Church – his work has the dignity and
force that is desperately needed today.' 'Well, yes', he replied,
catching the enthusiasm, 'and he would be very cheap.'[4]

Williamson told Hussey that Moore was primarily a sculptor
and a very good one, that he was coming down to Northampton the following week to judge a competition, and might be
willing to discuss the possibility of a commissioned work for
St Matthew's. Let Hussey take up the story again. 'Some days
later', he tells us,

I met Moore at supper in the Angel Hotel in Northampton.
Williamson had given him a brief outline of our conversation
and had taken him to see the church. In the course of the meal
I asked him whether he would be interested in the project;
he replied that he would, though whether it could go further,
whether he could and would want to do it, he just couldn't say
at present. I asked whether he would *believe* in the subject and
he replied 'Yes, I would. Though whether or not I should agree
with your theology, I just do not know. I think it is only through
our art that we artists can come to understand your theology.'[5]

In a subsequent letter to Hussey, Moore expanded on his doubts
as to whether he could produce a specific, and moreover religious, theme. 'Although I was very interested', he wrote,

I wasn't sure whether I could do it, or whether I even wanted
to do it. One knows that Religion has been the inspiration of
most of Europe's greatest painting and sculpture, and that the
Church in the past has encouraged and employed the greatest
artists; but the great tradition of religious art seems to have
got lost completely in the present day, and the general level
of church art has fallen very low (as anyone can see from the
affected and sentimental prettiness sold for church decoration
in church art shops.

'Therefore', he concludes,

I felt it was not a commission straightaway and light-heartedly
to agree to undertake, and I could only promise to make
notebook sketches from which I could do small clay models,
and only then should I be able to say whether I could produce
something which would be satisfactory as sculpture and also
satisfy my idea of the 'Madonna and Child' theme too.[6]

There are surely few verbal or written exchanges between artist
and patron in the history of religious art to address the relationship between art and theology and between idea and image,
with such immediacy, frankness and parity.

For Hussey, two courses of action were now necessary. One
was to encourage his father, now retired, to donate the Moore
'Madonna and Child' as his gift to St Matthew's on its jubilee.
Although Hussey was mildly apprehensive (his father could be
both irascible and aesthetically conservative, and 'I did not wish
him to give something he could not be happy about'), he was no
doubt relieved when his father responded that 'if it was what I
was convinced was right, and had taken the best advice about,
then he would be very happy'.[7]

The second task – to secure the approval of his Parochial Church Council – was potentially trickier. Here Hussey left little to chance. On the one hand he felt, as he told Moore, that 'the crucial stage would be the reaction of the Church Council to the models', and 'I would be loath to try to force through anything which the simple folk who use the church and who are represented by the Council, felt offended their religious susceptibilities.' Beneath such apparent, if somewhat paternalistic, sensitivities lay a more subtle subtext. As he confessed to Moore, 'something "not exactly what they would have chosen" or which they "could not quite understand", I do not think would matter, because they would be willing, with encouragement, I feel sure, to accept it and wait for its beauty to grow on them.'[8] On the other hand, back in 1942, Hussey was well aware that few of his parishioners were likely to have even heard of Henry Moore. Indeed they would have had other things on their minds! Hence he felt it was 'only fair' to give them informed opinions on the artist and the project.

Never a man to underplay his hand, Hussey chose three heavyweight witnesses. One, Kenneth Clark, then director of the National Gallery and already a celebrated connoisseur, wrote to him (after Hussey visited him in person) to say

> how much in sympathy I am with your idea that Henry
> Moore should do a Madonna and Child for your church.
> I consider him the greatest living sculptor and it is of the
> utmost importance that the Church should employ artists
> of first-rate talent instead of the mediocrities usually
> employed.[9]

A second was the widely known writer, art critic and radio broadcaster Eric Newton, who wrote in similar vein. The third was George Bell, Bishop of Chichester ('the only bishop I knew of', Hussey recalled later, 'who was very interested in the arts and might be sympathetic'), who wrote

> Mr Moore is one of the greatest living sculptors, and one of the most sensitive and sympathetic artists working today.... I do not think you could go wrong in commissioning him. I shall be much interested to hear how things go. How one longs for churches to give a lead in the revival of that association of religion and art which has meant so much to the whole religious and spiritual life of the country. If you are able to do this at St Matthew's in the way proposed you will be giving a lead which will in my judgement be of great value.[10]

Perhaps unsurprisingly, the Parochial Church Council 'almost unanimously' agreed to accept the gift from Hussey *père*, and chose the maquette they preferred. It was, in fact, the one that Moore himself thought the best, as it was slightly the more naturalistic.

As Moore began work in earnest, his own 'theological' reflections began to surface, not least in his letters to Hussey. They are worth repeating in full.

'There have been', he writes

> two particular motives or subjects which I've constantly used in my sculpture in the last 20 years – they are the 'Reclining Figure' idea and the 'Mother and Child' idea – (and perhaps of the two the 'Mother and Child' has been the more fundamental obsession). And I began thinking of the 'Madonna and Child' for St Matthew's by considering in what way a Madonna and

Child differs from a carving of just a 'Mother and Child' – that is by considering how in my opinion religious art differs from secular art.

'It's not easy', he continues,

to describe in words what this difference is, except by saying in general terms that the 'Madonna and Child' should have an austerity and a nobility and some touch of grandeur (even hieratic aloofness) which is missing in the 'everyday' 'Mother and Child' idea. From the sketches and little models I've done, the one we've chosen has I think a quiet dignity and gentleness. And I have tried to give a sense of complete easiness and repose, as though the Madonna could stay in the position for ever (as being in stone she will have to do). The Madonna is seated on a low bench, so that the angle formed between the nearly upright body and her legs is somewhat less than a right angle, and in this angle of her lap, safe and protected, sits the Infant. The Madonna's head is turned to face the direction where the statue is first seen walking down the aisle, whereas one gets the front view of the infant's head when standing directly in front of the statue … the 'Madonna and Child' will be slightly over life size. But I do not think it should be much over life size as the sculpture's real and full meaning is to be got only by looking at it from a more or less near view, and if from near-to it seemed too colossal it would conflict with the human feeling I'd like it to express.[11]

Today, over six decades after its installation, Moore's figure (*Figure 6*) owes its continuing impact not just to 'the quiet dignity and gentleness' that the sculptor was aiming at, but also to the careful siting of the group. The figure rests securely and calmly within the shell of the transept. The scale is beautifully adjusted to the expanse of wall between the windows and the floor. The Madonna's human gaze is towards the visitor as he or she moves down the nave. The child's gaze shares the nave and the sanctuary, poised, as it were, between the material and spiritual zones of the building.

However, back in 1944, immediate local reactions were far less sympathetic, and immediately after its unveiling (predictably, by Kenneth Clark) the statue was initially greeted, to judge from the correspondence columns of the local press (all carefully preserved by Hussey) with a mixture of hostility and hysteria.[12]

'I may be considered ignorant and unartistically minded', wrote one of his parishioners to the *Northampton Chronicle and Echo*,

> but I personally consider the Madonna and Child just unveiled in St Matthew's Church as an absolute insult to our intelligence. I always thought of the Madonna as a plain and gentle woman, and if this is an example of modern art I think it is as well to preserve the old ruins and monuments, lest posterity thinks 1944 art is a true conception of people's minds.

Another correspondent considered the piece

> an insult to every woman. But it is a grave insult to the one it is supposed to represent. The most beautiful works of art are now being destroyed and it is up to every good artist to try to replace them. But sacred subjects should be left alone, unless they can be portrayed in a real and proper manner. This one will disgust thousands of right-minded people.

A third letter (signed 'Simplicitas') combined sarcasm, theology and aesthetics in equal measure:

> As a tribute to Divine perfection, it has been thought fit to erect … a statue which, from its grotesque portrayal of the child

Jesus and His mother, must be repugnant as a 'monstrosity' to a majority of the parishioners. This sculpture may be great art without beauty, or it may be beautiful in the eyes of an initiated few, but it warps a mental picture of an ideal which has remained unchanged for 2,000 years.

A letter to the weekly *Northampton Independent*, headed 'A Monstrosity', went even further:

It was with disgust that I viewed the new statue of the Madonna and Child…. I cannot understand any sane 'artist' devoting time and trouble to the making of an image that strikes me as being out of all proportion and perspective. To my normal mind it is revolting. The churches are slipping from soul-saving to idolatry – man-made erections are becoming more important than the soul of man…. Hoping that this unfortunate piece of sculpture will be removed by public demand as soon as possible.

Walter Hussey, to his credit – and to our lasting benefit – was unfazed and unrepentant. His letter to Moore is worth repeating. Although his Madonna was 'not exactly what they [his parishioners] would have chosen or which they could not quite understand, I do not think this matters, because they would be willing, with encouragement I feel sure, to accept it, and wait for its beauty to grow on them in the future.'[13] Which is precisely what has happened.

Moore's sculpture was still unfinished when Hussey was already thinking 'that something was needed on the plain Bath stone wall of the south transept, to balance the Madonna and Child opposite in the North transept'. Indeed he raised the matter directly with Moore, who also thought that 'a picture would be best',[14] adding that 'I think that my friend Graham Sutherland would be the most suitable. Shall I invite him down to the unveiling of the Madonna and Child so that you can meet and discuss the matter with him?' Hence Sutherland came to the unveiling of the Moore, and was, as he describes it, 'bundled' into the south transept, where he asked Hussey whether he had any particular subject in mind. 'I replied' the latter recalls 'that I had vaguely thought of an "Agony in the Garden" because it could give some scope for landscape, and there seemed to me to be a relationship between his work and El Greco's. He said it was strange because one of the last things he had been doing was to copy El Greco's "Agony".' But 'of course' he added 'one's ambition would be to do a Crucifixion of significant size.' 'Well, that would be fine', Hussey responded, 'and it would admirably balance, in theme, the Madonna and Child in the opposite transept.'

The subsequent correspondence between Sutherland and Hussey (like that between Moore and Hussey) reveals a good deal of the artist's own approach to religious themes. Again it is worth citing some of it in full. 'The gulf', wrote Sutherland (who may well have seen for himself Hussey's collection of hostile letters to the local press), 'between the public and contemporary works has been too long and too wide. The difficulty has been that of the one not recognising the vitality and spiritual power of the other, and confusing unfamiliarity with what is thought to be ugliness.' 'With regard to our conversation in the church', he continues, 'I should welcome the opportunity to see what I could do. To do a religious painting of significant size has always been a wish at the back of my mind.' It remained at the back of his mind for the next six months, through pressure of other work, and Hussey's letters remained unanswered. But 'that is not to say', Sutherland finally wrote (in October 1944),

> that the problem of the 'Crucifixion' hasn't occupied me. I've thought about it a good deal while going about the trivial tasks of life and ... I begin to feel rather more fitted for the task, and certainly a great deal more closely approaching the mood and feeling necessary, than I would have done six months ago.
>
> It does seem to me that there are only two ways of approaching this subject. On the one hand a treatment detached, formal, hieratic(?) and impersonal. On the other, a (for want of better words) psychological or psychic and real (not necessarily naturalistic) treatment. I confess I incline towards the latter with all humility and great temerity ... That is not to say that the form of composition shouldn't have great formality. It should, since emotions in art must be crystallized and the moment frozen.

Nearly another eight months were to pass ('I am still very heavily engaged on war art.... and I hope this doesn't throw your plans out. I'm still as keen as ever') before Sutherland could write (on 30 May 1945):

> As for my painting: I'm still very absorbed by the idea of a Crucifixion. The very difficulties are fascinating. The very shape of the Cross has become a symbol so familiar that the Act it stands for must have become to many almost unreal. I would still like to try it; if my powers prove insufficient – and I can assure you that of all critics I shall be the most careful and severe – then, perhaps, I should fall back on the less difficult and less complex 'Way of the Cross, or Agony in the Garden'.

Over the same period, Hussey, for his part, was in the process of softening up his Parochial Church Council – although, of course, the Sutherland project, if not yet a formal commission, was already well under way. This time his tactics were slightly different. 'In putting the whole scheme before the Church Council', he tells us,

> I pointed to the need for some feature on the large blank wall in the south transept, drew attention to the appropriateness of the Crucifixion as a subject to balance the Madonna and child in the opposite transept, and told them that all my researches pointed to Graham Sutherland as the most suitable artist. I read them some passages from Hans Feibusch's then recent book on *Mural Painting*.[15]

These included the following exhortation: 'I should like to shake up both architects and painters to overcome the anaemia and whimsicality that have become a characteristic of mural painting … let churches be decorated by such men as Georges Rouault or Graham Sutherland', and the stern warning that

> there is another danger … that of talking baby language. To see the way some of our best church and cathedral builders decorate their work with nursery emblems, golden stars, chubby Christmas angels, lilies, lambs and shepherds, insipid sculptures and paintings of a silly, false naivety, one wonders in what world they live. The men who came home from the war, and all the rest of us, have seen too much horror and evil; when we close our eyes terrible sights haunt us; the world is seething with bestiality; and it is all man's doing. Only the most profound, tragic, moving, Sublime vision can redeem us. The voice of the Church should be heard above the thunderstorm; and the artist should be her mouthpiece.[16]

With his Council no doubt still reeling from these Feibusch passages, Hussey then read them, as with the Moore commission, supportive letters from Kenneth Clark and Eric Newton (both of whom had seen Sutherland's final sketch), and followed this up by explaining that 'they would be shown what Sutherland intended to do and it would be for them to decide whether they accepted it or not. This plan they agreed.' Hussey concluded this masterly exercise in guided democracy by then producing a monochrome photograph of the final 8 by 5 foot sketch. He records

> There was some sense of shock … but no hostility. Instead
> a thoughtful discussion and some questions. One articulate
> member commented curtly. 'This is one of the most disturbing
> and shocking pictures that I have seen; therefore I think it
> should go into the church.'[17]

This became more or less the general view and the picture was passed.

On 18 November 1946, the picture was unveiled by the ex-director of the Victoria and Albert Museum, Sir Eric Maclagan, who was also the son of a former Archbishop of York, and a close friend of the local magnate, Lord Spencer, who also chaired the Diocesan Advisory Board – clear evidence, if any more is needed, of Walter Hussey's formidable capacity for what, in modern jargon, would be called 'productive networking'. This time, although there were the usual letters of protest (all from outside the parish), there was no such outcry as that which greeted the Moore. Hussey's retrospective explanation is both perceptive and plausible. 'I think', he wrote in 1985,

> this was partly because it was the second modern work,
> but more because the 'distortions' in the Crucifixion had a
> more obvious psychological justification. It was a profoundly

disturbing work, but so also was the event that it predicted. It would be impossible to point to most modern representations of the Crucifixion – such as the small one in the top of the window above the picture, where the figure might almost be a ballet dancer in a pose – and to tell, for example, somebody who had been in Belsen concentration camp that Christ knew about and had experienced human suffering. The terrible pictures of the concentration camp had, indeed, first been published in *Picture Post* when Sutherland was thinking about the Crucifixion, and inevitably influenced him.[18]

The latter had, in fact, on emerging from the violence of his own experiences as a war artist, chosen – after some hesitation, as we have seen – to concentrate, at St Matthew's, on Christ's own great suffering, and the result remains a powerfully disturbing painting (*Figure 7*). It is one that has an integral place in the development of his style and his vision of the world. More important here is evidence of Sutherland's own personal transition from a primarily professional interest in the subject matter to his own religious identity. 'The theme of the Crucifixion had long been in my mind', he told the critic Pierre Jeannerat shortly after completing the St Matthew's commission. 'The only real difficulties I encountered were those of grappling with my own emotions and my own means of expression. I think I have succeeded, and might even now be described as a "religious" man.'[19]

Walter Hussey's own creative energy was, in its own way, as remarkable as that of those he cajoled, championed and commissioned in the service of the Church. As Kenneth Clark – a leading supporter – once said of him, 'if he had not been in holy orders he would have been a great impresario',[20] and he certainly possessed the aesthetic self-confidence, enthusiasm and sheer nerve that enabled him to promote Moore and Sutherland, not to mention Britten (whose wonderful cantata 'Rejoice in the Lamb' was composed for the Patronal Festival at St Matthew's in 1943), at a time when all three were members of a widely criticised avant-garde. In doing so he also helped to revive a once great tradition of religious art among contemporary artists. As Peter Pears wrote to Hussey in 1940, 'if only all Vicars had been so understanding as you are.... I don't believe the Church would have lost so many of her artist sons.'[21] He also had the wealth, connections and motivation ('the nature of God cannot be confined within verbal definitions', he once said) that made his priestly patronage – especially if his Deanship of Chichester is added to his incumbency in Northampton – unparalleled in modern times. The French Dominican, Père Couturier (trained as an artist himself, and the patron and friend of Braque, Léger, Matisse, Picasso and Rouault, among others), is, of course, the outstanding exception. His church at Assy and the Matisse Chapel at Vence are both now centres of pilgrimage and part of twentieth-century art history in a way that a church in suburban Northampton is not. Yet the parallel histories of all three are not merely about inspired patronage, but more essentially, as this case study has tried to illustrate (largely through the leading protagonists' own words), also about the highly complex nexus of patron, artist, parish, community and society that is so often integral to the making of religious art, yesterday and today.

5

holy places and hollow spaces

The three preceding chapters provided case studies of religious art in a specific historical context, a modern exhibition setting, and in response to inspired clerical patronage. The present one is concerned more with religious buildings themselves, not merely as works of art, but as vehicles for personal and communal experience and belief. How far is such a building what W.B. Yeats called 'the artifice of eternity',[1] through which the numinous is disclosed without the ritual processes that are so often involved? How far does it fulfil what the late-Victorian church architect Sir Ninian Comper described as its primary purpose – 'to move to worship, to bring a man to his knees, to refresh the soul in a weary land'?[2]

The answers are, inevitably, highly complex, whatever disciplinary – or interdisciplinary – perspectives are adopted. One, perhaps the broadest, and also the most banal, would argue that those sites already deemed 'holy' or 'sacred' – Avebury, the Dome of the Rock, Mount Fuji, Assisi – are likely to be perceived, and experienced, as such by those who visit them. Here some personal sense of the numinous is almost a self-fulfilling prophecy, or at least a cognitive presupposition. This is especially the case at most pilgrimage sites within the major religious traditions, although pilgrimage itself can take many different phenomenological forms. Nonetheless, as Reader and Walter put it, 'pilgrimage sites, whether categorised as sacred places or not … provide a *tabula rasa* upon which the visitor can decipher or inscribe his or her own perceptions', and they argue convincingly that shrines and holy places acquire their power through their 'ability to reflect and absorb a multiplicity of religious discourses, to be able to offer a variety of clients what each of them desires'.[3] In this sense, not least within the Christian tradition, church buildings can provide a 'sacred canopy' (both literally and metaphorically), a significant place and space within which the individual is able to find meaning, and, in Victor Turner's telling phrase, 'achieve liminal experience – to move beyond the psychic constraints of a mundane existence, to step out of time and attain new, larger perspectives'.[4]

Put differently, and in plainer language, such buildings can serve as a psychological resource. As self-explanatory monuments to the historical continuity of Western Christendom, they lead us back to a world we have lost – a deep wellspring of residual religiosity upon which we can therapeutically draw – and delivering an emotional and spiritual pay-off which is far less evident in secular buildings of the same era. Indeed they represent something beyond, and above, the merely secular.

A second approach to understanding the 'religious' consequences of religious buildings for individuals is more overtly architectural than anthropological in emphasis. Here one theorist is particularly relevant. John Renard,[5] an American specialist in Islamic art and architecture, suggests that religious architecture functions on at least three levels – the *communitarian*, the *didactic* and the *experiential* (a taxonomy that resonates closely with that relating to religious art per se in our first chapter). He suggests that 'taken together these levels encompass the meaning and message communicated by the sum of a building's formal qualities'. The *communitarian* level relates to historical context, to ritual, and to the role of a built form as a place that fosters community and responds to that community's spiritual and temporal needs. Numerous historical and cultural variations are involved. The *didactic* function relates, in its turn, to the role of explicit symbolism in projecting the content of a religion. Through their structure and ornamentation, Renard argues, religious buildings 'communicate ... at least five aspects of a religious community's fundamentals: ritual practice, cosmology, sense of liturgical time, view of community history, and the notion of correspondence between microcosm and macrocosm'. One of these is of particular relevance to our own discussion. It is his suggestion that such architecture not only teaches about a tradition's cosmology ('its larger sense of the cosmos as sacred space, through the characteristics of siting, orientation, and structural symbolism') but also that 'a particular tradition "constructs" its own cosmos'. His argument here has strong echoes of Rudolf Otto's general contention (aired, of course, by romantic theorists two centuries before Otto) that 'the most effective means of conveying an experience of the sacred is to communicate a sense of the sublime', with the rider that 'architecture is the most apt medium for that purpose'.[6] He may well be right. As the philosopher (and religious sceptic) George Santayana once wrote of King's College Chapel, 'never was perspective more magnetic or vault more alive. We are in the presence of something magical, something sublime.'[7]

Renard's final category for evaluating the impact of religious artefacts upon people – the experiential – is in one sense the most psychologically self-evident. Arguing (perhaps somewhat gratuitously) that 'so many aspects of the built environment are capable of eliciting intense emotion', and drawing directly upon Otto's notion of 'creature feeling', which the latter describes as 'the emotions of a creature, submerged and overwhelmed by its own nothingness in contrast to that which is supreme above all creatures', he suggests that a wide range of what he calls 'experiential intangibles' can be invoked through 'the manipulation of formal characteristics such as line, space, mass, surface, colour, proportion, movement, rhythm and light'. Such visual strategies would have been wholly intelligible to, for example, Abbot Suger, or Borromini or Butterfield. But where Renard is especially illuminating is in devising four distinct continua along which to 'place' major architectural forms in relation to religious experience. The first runs from the simple to the pluriform. In terms of a building's ground plan, some sacred architecture is starkly simple and uncluttered, such as many early Nonconformist meeting houses, or neighbourhood mosques or the Rothko chapel. Such spaces can, Renard argues, establish a mood of repose and quiet.

Other sacred spaces can offer, in contrast, 'a luxuriant proliferation of subsidiary spaces, side-altars and images' which makes an immediate impact on the visitor and 'can induce a feeling of intense activity and high energy'. Baroque cathedrals with many side chapels, each devoted to a saint or devotional conception of the deity, firmly occupy this end of the continuum.

A second continuum, for Renard, runs from the hidden and private to the open and public. At one end are classic Hindu temples, which use the metaphor of the womb chamber (*garbhagriha*) to describe their holy of holies, while within the Christian tradition the most hidden and private might be Orthodox churches that maintain strict use of the iconostasis as a screen between ritual action and the congregation, while congregational style churches – with one large undifferentiated gathering space – would occupy the opposite end of the continuum. A third, related, continuum would run from interiority to exteriority, corresponding closely to darkness and light, while a fourth, final, one is that from 'the more massive and sculpted to the more delicate and architectonic'. Some spaces (the fortress churches of the Languedoc or Trinity Episcopal Church in Boston,[8] for example) convey an overwhelming sense of massiveness and gravity. They do not, in Renard's judgement, 'so much *construct* a space as *open* one up, evoking a sense of primaeval naturalness and organic integrity'. Towards the other end of this continuum lies the Gothic cathedral, and many major parish churches which successfully convey a feeling of what Renard calls 'heaven-seeking refinement of structure'.

In sum, this concept of 'experiential function' is a useful way of describing what might, in religious terms, happen to anyone entering a particular architectural space: it also helps to explain why such changes happen. Similarly, the communitarian function relates to what both believers and non-believers alike (and those in between) do in such a space, while the didactic focuses on what, if anything, they might actually learn there. Although Renard's own perspective might seem both overschematic and architecturally overdetermined, it is also highly consonant with much of the relatively meagre British research conducted to date on visitor responses to sacred space. At Canterbury Cathedral, for example, Christopher Lewis[9] reports that while visitors claimed to be there 'for themselves' or as 'enquiring individuals', they also found that the building itself (whose 'size' and 'atmosphere' were most frequently alluded to in their completed questionnaires) was above all an 'accessible' and 'significant' space. As Lewis puts it, 'here … anyone may come in and then graze at will, reflecting, lighting a candle [indeed English demand for candles in churches all but doubled between the late 1980s and late 1990s] and praying'.

Elsewhere, visitor responses to sacred space have been amusingly, but acutely, described by staff at one major civic church as falling into four distinct patterns of behaviour. First there are the *streakers* perambulating at speed to ensure maximum site coverage while searching for specific visual trophies – a memorial tablet to a minor poet, a sculptural figure, a fragment of wall painting. Then there are the *strollers* who move more slowly through the same visual terrain, walking haphazardly, even unpredictably, towards specific spaces and objects, and with a relatively limited attention span. They are not to be confused with either *grazers* (a term also used by Lewis), who roam through specific meadows – a chantry chapel, medieval or Burne Jones glass, or misericorded choir stalls – devouring every significant, and sometimes insignificant, detail, or with *readers* who, church guidebook or Pevsner in hand, occasionally lift their eyes from the printed page to give the listed items their undivided, if temporary, attention.

Such visible patterns of behaviour seem psychologically – and phenomenologically – far removed from Renard's 'experiential' categories noted earlier. This may be partly due to their Anglican context, in which the ecclesiology of Protestantism contains little or no theology of 'place'. As Martyn Percy has shrewdly remarked. 'For Protestants, God is within, or in the midst of the praises of his people. Linking God to a place is too constraining and routinized.… God is a mind–heart–body experience in most strands of Protestantism; little value is put on buildings, aesthetics or shrines.'[10] Nonetheless one final type of perceived visitor response, recently noted by observers in a major English city church, merits special attention. These are what they came to call the *sniffers*. Here, individuals, upon entering the church, would metaphorically – and sometimes literally – sniff the atmosphere, trying to sense the presence or absence of (or potential for) the numinous, the holy, of 'something there', even the Christian God Himself. Here they were empirically testing whether they were in fact entering what Nicholas Lash has called 'a hollow space' rather than a 'holy place'[11] – or vice versa. Here, too, they were echoing, in many respects, the position adopted by the contemporary French theologian Daniel Bourgeois,[12] who has long argued that medieval Christian architecture (his own specialism), 'far from attempting to represent the unrepresentable, renders visible the presence of the sacred through the very disposition of the architectural elements … these show how the ineffable Deity inhabits the created world'. Behind this lies an even broader supposition. 'The object of architecture', he contends,

> is not a material thing (a house, a church) but a human activity, the act of dwelling … true architectural creation renders visible the deeper meaning of the act of dwelling. Distinct from mere artistic form, visuality is a special property of architectural objects which ensures that buildings, particularly religious buildings, embody a social and spiritual message.

Yet in our own time such a message is far from clear, or even predictable. The signals are both contradictory and confusing. It is not merely that, as the social anthropologists Coleman and Collins have argued, 'while the physical structures and perspectives of major sacred sites are frequently designed to suggest authoritative narrative to worshippers, their messages may be deliberately or inadvertently misread by individuals or groups of believers'.[13] It is also that in practice (as opposed to the theoretical perspectives outlined earlier in this chapter) we continue to know very little about what 'physical structures and perspectives' – let alone their contents – really suggest to believer and unbeliever alike. We may, of course, recall Eliot's injunction, at Little Gidding, to 'kneel where prayer has been valid', or picture Larkin, 'Hatless, I take off my cycle-clips in awkward reverence,/ Move forward, run my hand around the font', but more substantial evidence of precisely *when* and *how* people's primary religious experiences are mediated through such built forms continues to prove elusive.

The second difficulty, although less methodologically taxing, is equally intractable. Here the figures speak for themselves. In 2004, the English Tourist Board[14] estimated that 68.7 million visits were made to historic properties in England. Cathedrals and churches accounted for about 32.4 million of these – nearly half the total – of which 14.6 million were to Anglican cathedrals. Such figures are startling, especially when compared with statistics for regular attendance at places of worship (where 'regular' means once a month or more often). These, depending on which survey is drawn upon, averaged out in 2004 at between 6 and 7 per cent of the adult population. In short, while British – and especially English – public observance is contracting, church, and especially cathedral, *visiting* is expanding, perhaps as never before. How do we begin to explain this phenomenon?

One explanation, already hinted at earlier in this chapter, is that many religious buildings have now become sites of essentially *secular* pilgrimage – related to the desired therapeutic, leisure, cultural and occasionally spiritual goals of the pilgrim. As Kieran Flanagan puts it, 'increasingly, those who stroll around cathedrals and churches do so as outsiders'[15] and 'few in present culture devote themselves sufficiently to seeing the unseen to be able to discern the cultural and symbolic capital of these richly laden edifices'.[16] Indeed the latter, far from providing 'religious space' of potentially transcendental significance, are now – *pace* Renard – reduced to little more than the ecclesiastical branch of the heritage industry. Hence a second, somewhat Bourdieu-like, explanation for the marked differential between recorded visiting and worship figures suggests itself. It is that in an age of mass tourism, the motor car, and above all where there has been a shift in the developed world from mass production to mass consumption as the primary form of economic activity, what some churches (and especially cathedrals) now offer is what could be described as 'the total church experience', packaged and commodified in the manner of a theme park attraction. Or if liturgical music is relentlessly piped into every sacred space, then the 'theme park' metaphor could be changed to what Martyn Percy has described (only half-mischievously) as 'A Spiritual Car Wash, where believer and non-believer alike can be brushed, sprayed and soaked with the anointing power of God as they pass through.'[17]

A third, more overtly cultural-historical, explanation for such high church visiting figures might well be that many of England's cathedrals and parish churches (unlike those in France or even the Netherlands, for example), are irretrievably embedded within a cultural tradition defined by one of its historians, Robert Hewison, as 'retrospective, nostalgic and entropic'.[18] In this sense – as what William Morris called 'sacred monuments of the nation's growth and hope'[19] – they embody Englishness both literally and symbolically. Indeed they are as nationalistic

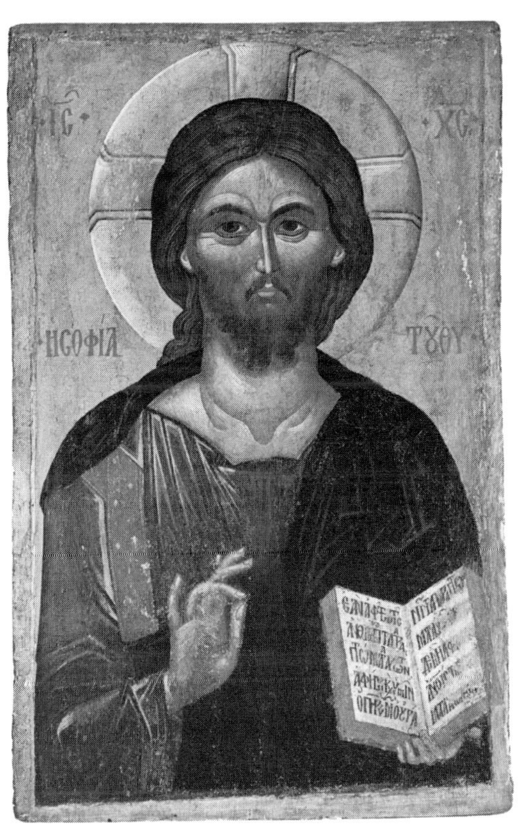

FIGURE 1 Icon of Christ the Divine Wisdom. Fourteenth-century school of Salonika. Athens, Byzantine Museum.

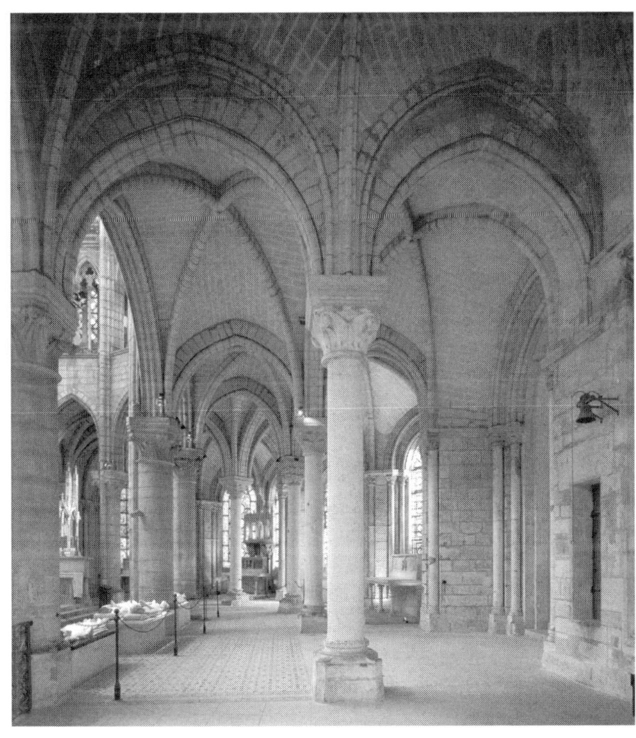

FIGURE 2 St Denis Abbey, Ambulatory, 1140–44.

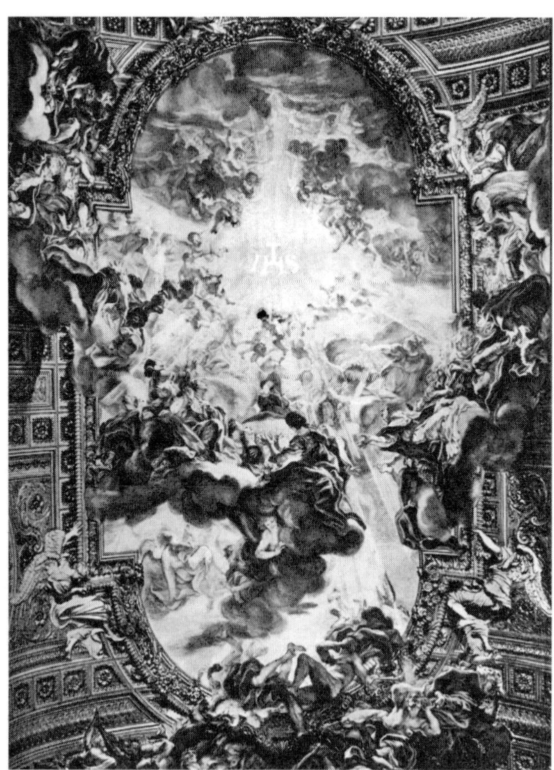

FIGURE 3   Francesco Gaulli ('Baccicio'), 'The Adoration of the Holy Name of Jesus', 1668–85. Ceiling of Il Gesu, Rome.

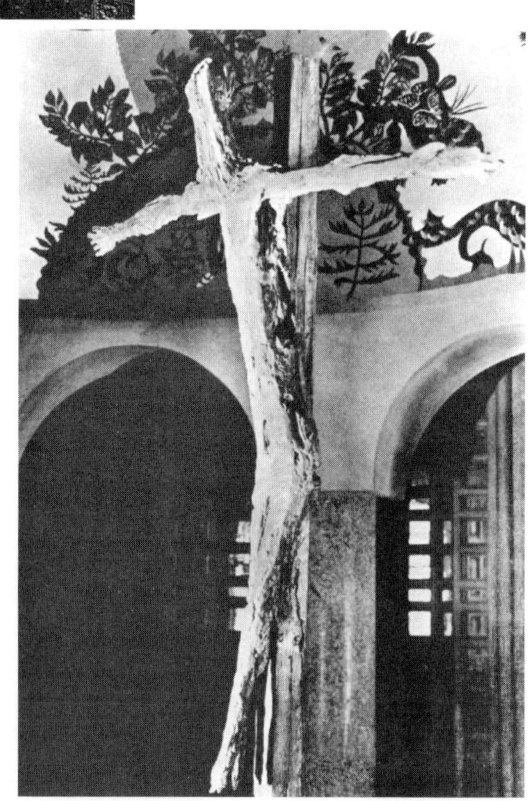

FIGURE 4   Germaine Richier, crucifix bronze, 1950. Cast in situ, Assy, France.

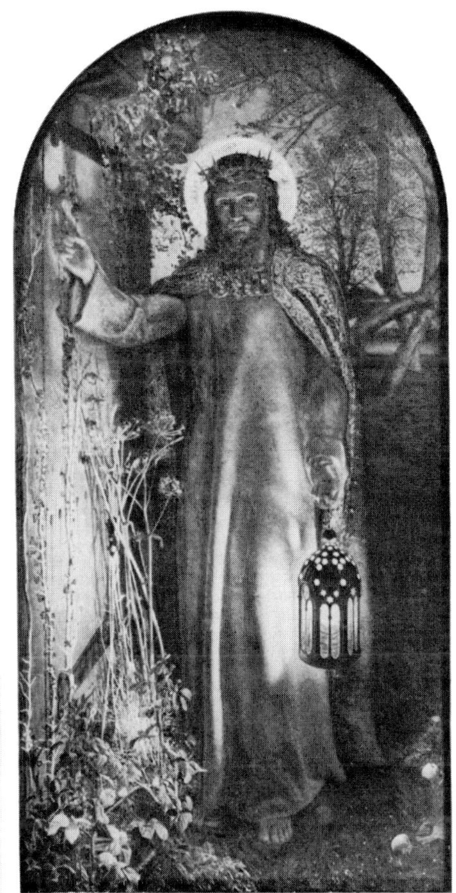

FIGURE 5   Holman Hunt,
'The Light of the World', 1851–53.
Keble College, Oxford.

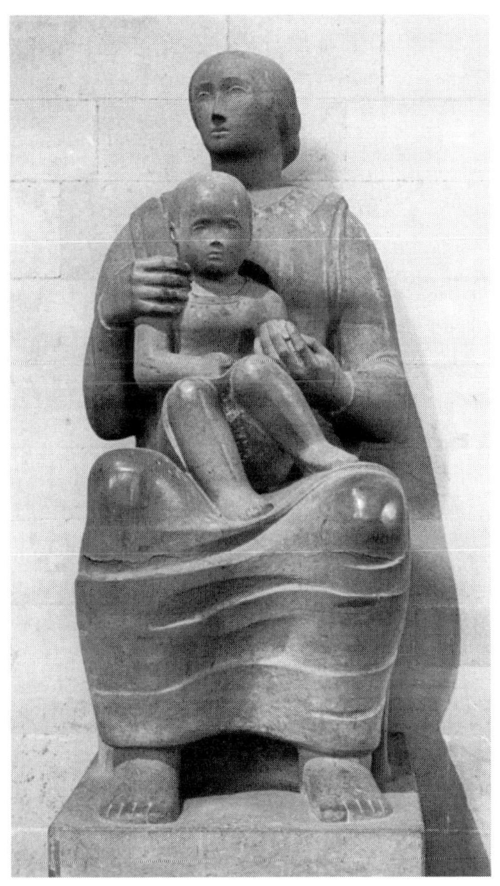

FIGURE 6   Henry Moore,
'Madonna and Child', 1943–44.
St Matthew's Church, Northampton.

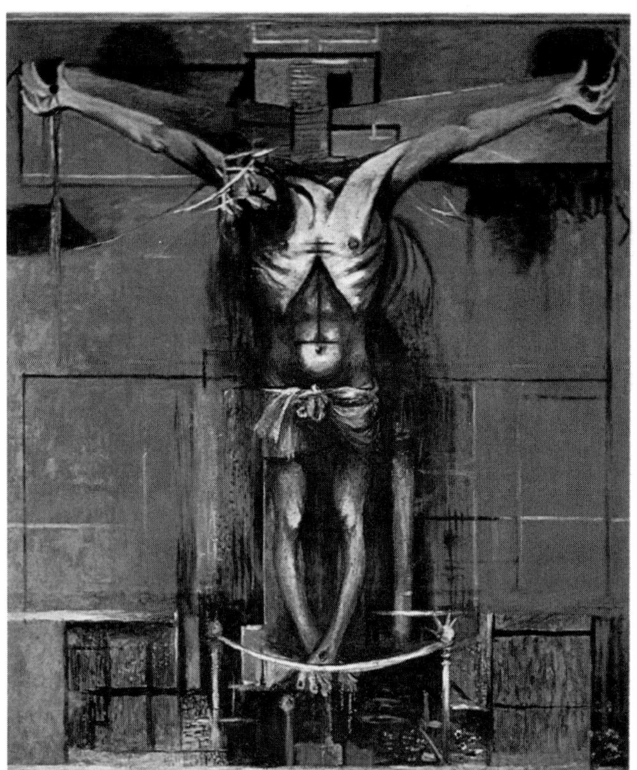

FIGURE 7
Graham Sutherland,
'Crucifixion', 1946.
St Matthew's Church,
Northampton.

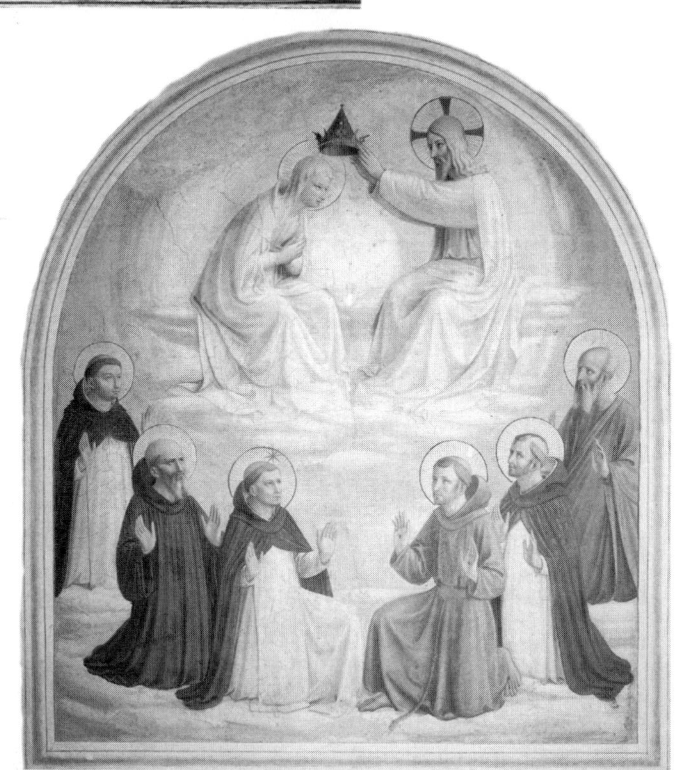

FIGURE 8
Fra Angelico,
'Coronation of the
Virgin', c. 1445.
San Marco, Florence.

FIGURE 9   Henri Matisse,
Chapelle du Rosaire,
Vence, 1948.

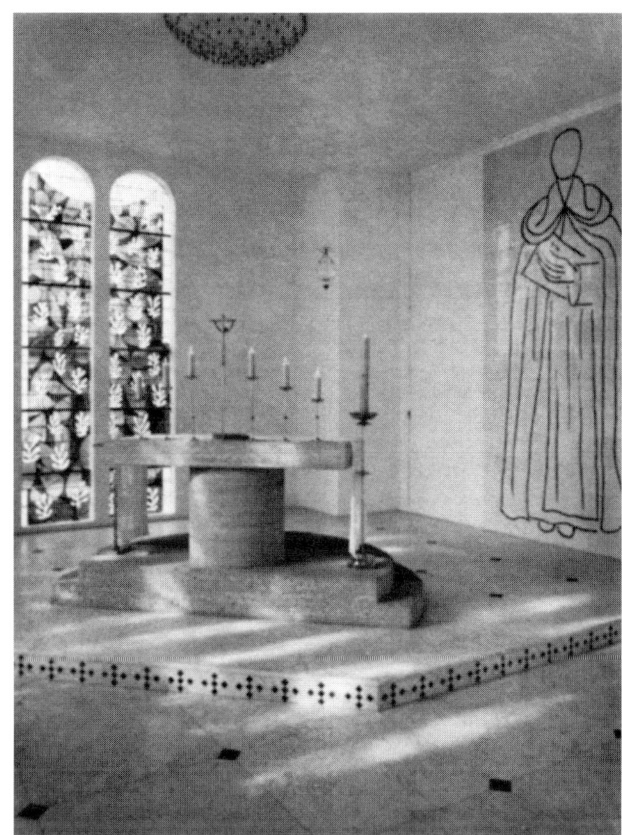

FIGURE 10
Mark Rothko, chapel,
with original skylight
grid, 1971. Houston, Texas.

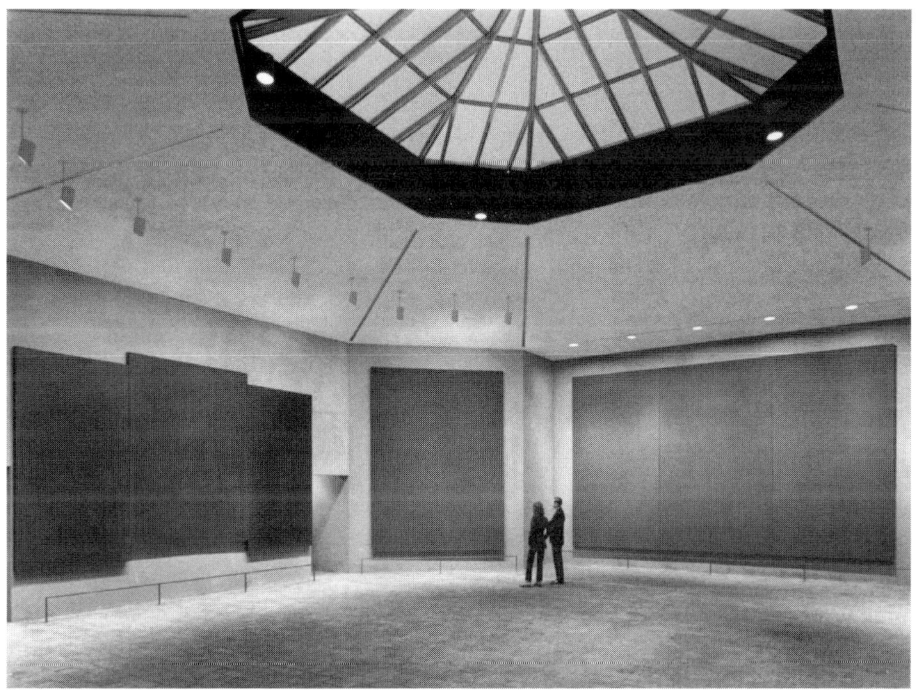

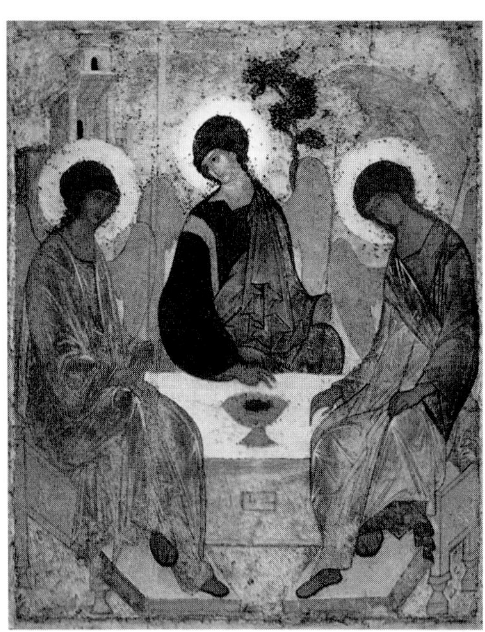

FIGURE 11   Andrei Rublev,
Old Testament Trinity, 1411.
Tretyakov Gallery, Moscow.

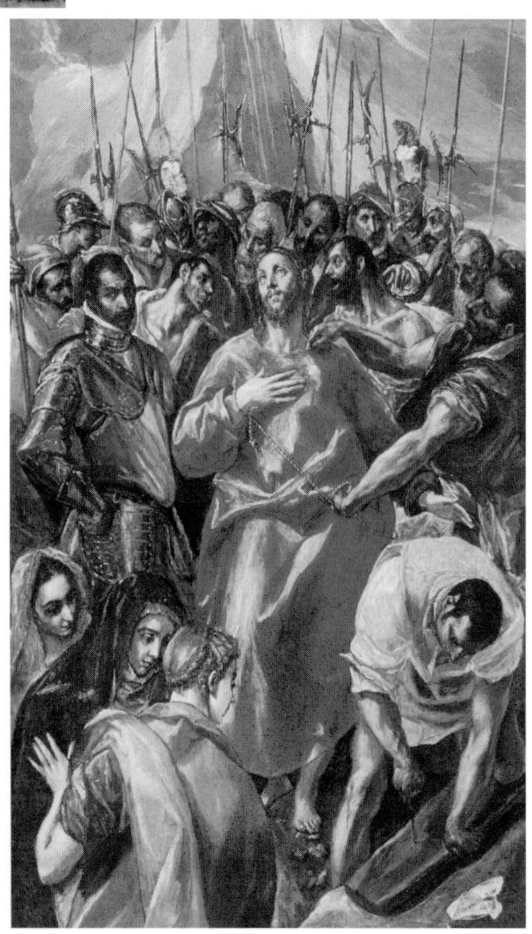

FIGURE 12   El Greco,
'The Disrobing of Christ'
('El Espolio'), 1577–79.
Bearsted Collection,
Upton House (National Trust)

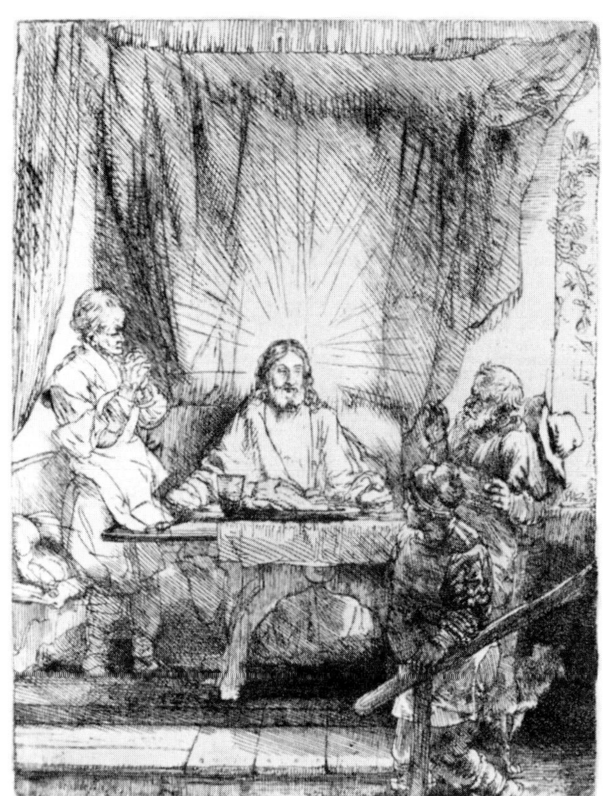

FIGURE 13 Rembrandt van Rijn, 'The Supper at Emmaus', etching, 1654. Paris, Louvre.

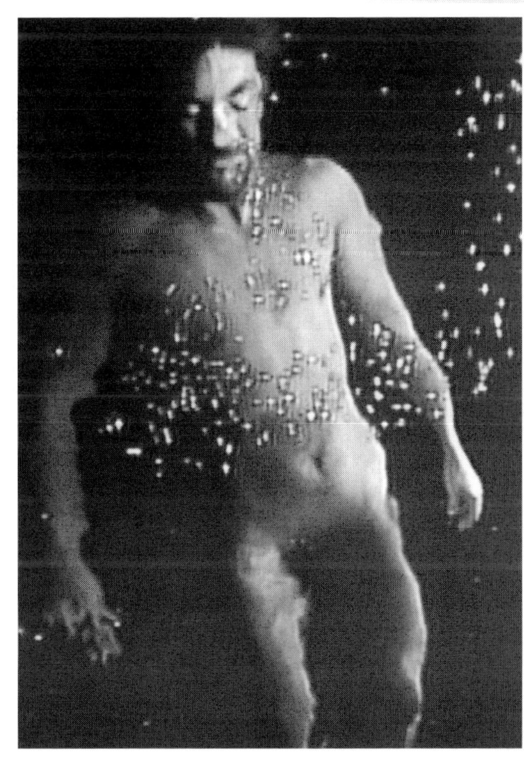

FIGURE 14 Bill Viola, 'The Messenger', video/sound installation, 1996.

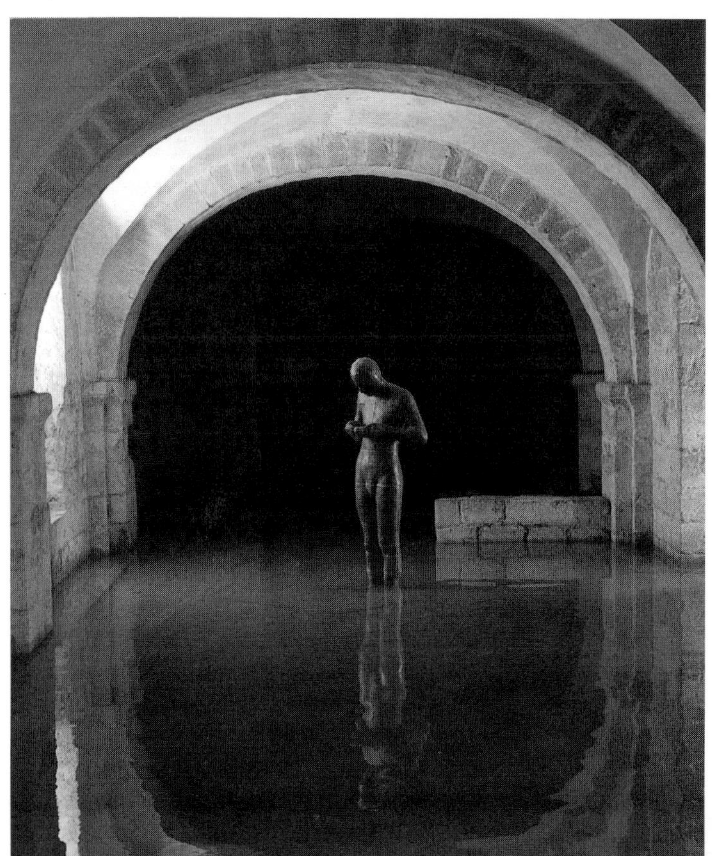

FIGURE 15
Anthony Gormley,
'Sound II', 1986.
Winchester
Cathedral,
crypt.

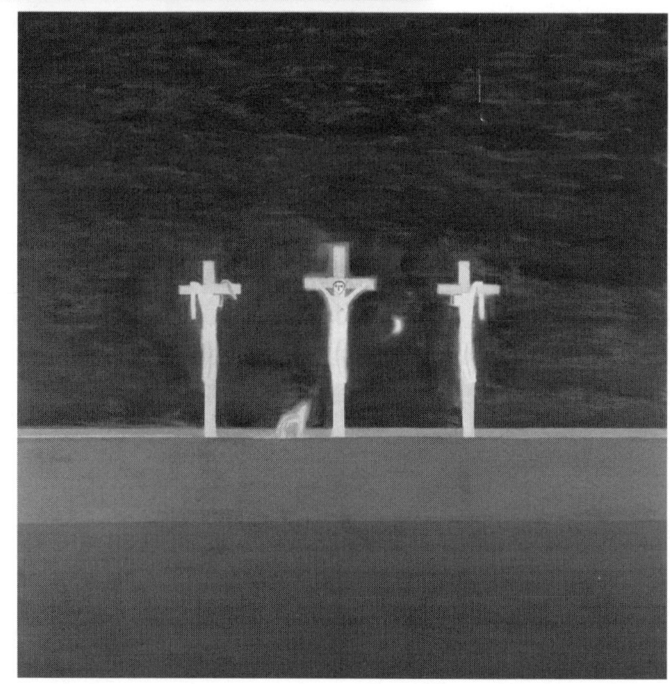

FIGURE 16
Craigie Aitchison,
'Calvary', 1998.
Liverpool Cathedral.

as a Shinto shrine (which some Japanese call 'the soul of our nation'), while also serving as self-explanatory monuments to the historical continuity of English Christianity, and as powerful if residual symbols of a now-vanished religiosity. One could perhaps go even further here and suggest that at a time of much national self-doubt and uncertainty (about involvement in Iraq or closer engagement with Europe, for example) religious buildings can act as a permanent wellspring of historicism and nostalgia upon which we can always therapeutically draw. In this sense they can deliver an emotional and spiritual pay-off far more potent than any derived from most secular buildings, however ancient or famous.

All three explanations, separately and together, carry powerful consequences for the present and future relationship between aesthetic and religious experience, especially as mediated through religious architecture. One is that many traditionally 'sacred' spaces are becoming progressively *desacralised*, in whatever continent or religious tradition they are located. Global tourism (pilgrimage's final historical mutation) rather than global unbelief, has seen to that. In such a context the conviction of the Indian Christian writer and artist Jyoti Sahi (in his brilliant book *Holy Ground*) that the church as a built form remains a – possibly *the* – physical expression of incarnational theology, although deeply felt and strongly argued, is not entirely persuasive. For example, in a passage which could have been penned by Abbot Suger himself, he writes:

> the building serves as a door through which the divine reality
> is experienced as entering first into the cosmos, and then

through the cosmos and nature as we experience it with our bodily senses into the very heart and physical self-awareness of the worshipper.[20]

Yet so often today, in the West as well as in Sahi's India, our apprehension of 'divine reality' is subverted by the stuttering of digital cameras, the murmur of auto-guides, the rustle of green Michelins and the relentless tinkle of the cash register. Any possibility of even approaching, let alone experiencing, God Incarnate is invariably denied us. So, too, is not merely our sense of the ordering of sacred space, but our very sense of the sacred itself.

A second consequence, not unconnected with the first, is what might be described as the 'uncoupling' of visual and religious experience within a single space. The process is not a wholly new one. In William Dean Howell's novel *A Hazard of New Fortunes* (1890) the hero, Basil March, and his wife visit New York's then fashionable Grace Episcopal Church (built 1843). As Bostonians, they are both impressed and a little ashamed of their reaction to its Puginesque splendour.

> Rapt far from New York, if not from earth, in the dim richness
> of the painted light, the hallowed music took them with
> solemn ecstasy; the aerial, aspiring Gothic forms seemed to
> lift them heavenward. They came out reluctant into the dazzle
> and bustle of the street, with a feeling that they were too good
> for it.... 'But no matter how consecrated we feel now' he said
> 'we mustn't forget that we went into the church for precisely
> the same reason that we went to the Vienna Café for break-
> fast – to satisfy an aesthetic sense.... It was a purely pagan
> impulse.'[21]

In our own time this process of deconsecration is all but complete. It is not necessarily the product of secularisation per se – where visual gratification has supplanted transcendental expectation – although in a recent cathedral survey only 20 per cent of those questioned stated a 'specifically religious' interest in their visit. Nor is it simply that for many, furnishings such as font, altar, screen, rood and piscina are perceived as 'beautiful' yet devoid of any religious resonance or meaning – part of a wider contemporary paradox whereby in a highly visual culture, Christian imagery has itself become increasingly invisible. It is, rather, part of a broader cultural *bouleversement* where, as André Malraux had already remarked in 1953, 'Once a mere collection, the art museum is by way of becoming a sort of shrine, the only one of the modern age.'[22] This in itself is, of course, a highly complex mutation. It is also one where, as the American cultural historian David Lowenthal suggests, declining religious belief has supplied the most essential backdrop. 'Now', he writes,

> large numbers of men and women, perhaps the majority, no longer believe that their innermost souls are known intimately by a caring God. So … far more of them than ever before seek for their 'authentic' selves in cherished landscapes, or family history, or the cultural artefacts of their kind…. And, of course, once they cease believing that eternity is their future and only significant heritage, men and women will place more emphasis not just on striving to enjoy themselves in the present, but also on revivifying the past. Because what else do they have?[23]

Although his thesis lacks cultural specificity, and bypasses the current global upswing in Christian fundamentalism, the phenomenon he identifies clearly has an impact on current responses to sacred spaces. Simon Jenkins's immensely popular guide *England's Thousand Best Churches* is both a product and a symptom of this. In his Introduction he remarks, with a kind of world-weary waspishness, how 'I have lost count of the number of church guides which assert "This building is not a museum, it is a place of worship"', and he goes on to say: 'I disagree. A church is a museum, and should be proud of the fact.' For him,

> An English church is more than a place of denominational worship. It is the stage on which the pageant of community has been played out for a millennium. The Church of England is the true Museum of England, and its buildings should be more treasured as a result.[24]

One can almost hear the English Heritage plaques being riveted into place! Such a stance inevitably conveys, indeed generates, for the nearly two million users of Jenkins' guide, a highly constricted view of what the ritual and credal context of a church building might actually be. For Jenkins 'a church is not a place of revealed truth, but rather a shrine of impenetrable mystery', and he seems unable, or unwilling, to conceive of it as both. Instead he seems content to regard religion as no more than a trace element or historical residue within the built form itself. 'For me', he writes, the experience is not of faith, but rather of the memory of faith present in an old building.'[25]

Such a stance does not only help to firmly relocate existing sacred spaces firmly within museum rather than ecclesiastical culture, where they become desacralised, psychologically deconsecrated, tourist sites. It was Picasso, rather than André

Malraux, who in 1951 described the church at Assy as 'no more than a superbly decorated museum'.[26] Over fifty years later it may also be the case that the art museum itself (to judge from the crowds thronging Tate Modern, especially on a Sunday) has now become the West's most sacralised institution – a ritual site, 'a temple where', as a former curator of the Louvre (Germaine Bazin), describes it, 'Time seems suspended. The visitor enters it in the hope of finding one of those momentary cultural epiphanies that give him the illusion of knowing intuitively his essence and his strengths.'[27] Viewed more anthropologically, it may well be the case that in the predominantly post-Christian West we too, as in other cultures and epochs, continue to build sites that publicly represent our beliefs about the order of the world, its past and present, and the individual's place within it. Today, these are more typically museums than houses of God. Theologically, too, it would seem that nowadays our museums (even those displaying religious art) aim to symbolise and embody secular truths which are rational and verifiable, and which have become normative and authoritative, while religion, although guaranteed as a matter of freedom and choice, has kept its authority only for voluntary believers, and often primarily within the private rather than the public domain. The implications for religious architecture are potentially profound. Crude triumphalism – whether Gothic, Baroque or High Victorian – is likely to be perceived both as redundant symbolism and as a symbol of institutional redundancy. Indeed the main features of postmodern culture – highly individualised, fissiparous and fractured, where beliefs themselves are pluralist, provisional and personalised – surely suggest the need to design and develop built forms that are either more resonant of the 'cellular' structures of the Early Church, or, as in the case of the Buddhist or Shinto *butsudan* in many Japanese homes, no more than a single, unconsecrated sacred space within the home. 'Holy places' rather than 'hollow spaces'.

6

artists, institutions and faith

Alert readers may have already noted that much of the discussion so far has yet to be conducted within a broader, overtly art-historical historical framework. This is partly because the hard evidence for any triangulation between a specific religious context, the beliefs and practices of a particular artist, and the art he or she produces often exists – where it exists at all – within the artwork itself rather than in personal memoranda or in remarks recorded by contemporaries. Even major primary sources – such as Vasari, or the *Farington Diary*, for example – or secondary reference works such as Elizabeth Gilmore Holt's *Documentary History of Art*, and most recently the 34-volume Macmillan *Dictionary of Art* (the art-historical equivalent of the musicians' *Grove*) pay comparatively scant attention to this triangulation. It is also because in so many cases the precise relationship between an artist's professional identity and their religious identity remains essentially covert rather than overt, implicit rather than explicit, and in some cases virtually non-existent.

None the less, while such sub-Ruskinian dicta (both drawn, in fact, from twentieth-century sources!) as 'religion is integral to art and art to religion' or that 'all art, arguably, involves an encounter with the mysterious and the invisible' are perhaps too simplistic and culturally redundant to convince many today, it is clear that the history of art and the history of religion are often intertwined. Hence it would be relatively easy to provide an unashamedly linear account of this interaction. In the West it might begin in the caves of Lascaux or with Stonehenge, where art was essentially linked to magic and ritual. It could then point to art's crucial role in expressing and sustaining the dynastic theocracies of Ancient Egypt, the charter myths and mystery religions of the Greeks, and the civil religion of both Republican and Imperial Rome. The place of rudimentary iconography in shaping the religious (and social) identity of Early Christians is well established, and the centrality of Imago Dei to the Iconoclastic controversy is exceptionally well documented. From the eleventh to the fourteenth century the intellectual, theological and institutional elisions of art and religion throughout medieval Christendom were integral to both Church and State, and to lord and peasant alike. The aesthetic consequences – from a single Romanesque capital to a free-standing Gothic cathedral, from stained glass to jewel-encrusted reliquary – were often spectacular.

Similarly the style and thematic content of much Renaissance art, both north and south of the Alps, owed as much to Christian as to classical, pagan sources, while many of its greatest visual triumphs – the Arena Chapel, San Marco, the Sistine – are unintelligible without reference to their ecclesiastical provenance. The Protestant Reformation, too, brought with it not only iconoclastic excess, and the destruction of religious art objects, but also a new visual aesthetic of its own, powerfully articulated in the work of Cranach and Dürer, for example.

The Baroque, although a highly variegated and diffuse cultural movement, was, as we have already noted, intrinsically linked to the Counter-Reformation project, to colonial mission, and to the use of art and architecture not only for liturgical and educational purposes but also to generate primary religious experience. From the early eighteenth century, however, other powerful intellectual forces such as Enlightenment rationalism, and the Romantic movement, in Europe and beyond, began to modify the 'traditional' interdependence of art, artist and religion, and art itself became an increasingly autonomous cult, with the artist as its votive functionary, unlicensed jester, or alienated outsider. At the same time the growth, throughout the nineteenth century, of both secularism and religious scepticism as a value, and secularisation as a process, further weakened the already fragile formal ties between art and religion in general, and, in particular, the interaction between religious art, its patrons and its practitioners in much of the post-Christian West until the present day. Indeed if contemporary postmodernity, with its attendant relativism and cultural fragmentation, is now as pervasively normative as some perceive it to be, then the future role of both religious art and those who make it may be one of increasing cultural marginality, trivialisation, and even virtual extinction.

Such a historical trajectory as that briefly outlined above is, although necessarily overcompressed and undernuanced, one way of 'positioning' the lives and works of individual artists conventionally characterised as 'religious' in either outlook or output – or both. It sees them not as divinely inspired, nor as jobbing craftsmen capitalising on fluctuating demand (although clearly some artists saw themselves primarily in such terms) but rather as persons caught up at the crucial points of intersection between religion, art and their own personal and professional identity as artist. Some specific art-historical scenarios may clarify this approach in more detail.

For example, it is clear from Barbara Raw's fascinating monograph *Anglo-Saxon Crucifixion Iconography and the Art of the Monastic Revival*[1] that the unknown craftsmen who painted and carved crucifixion scenes for the Anglo-Saxon church were more than mere artisans working under strict ecclesiastical control. Indeed, like some of the Pre-Raphaelites later (especially Holman Hunt), they were highly sensitised to current theological fashion. Indeed, as Raw shows, their primary visual motif – emphasising the link between Christ's death and Resurrection – served to shape as well as reflect current notions of redemption among clergy and laity alike. There was clearly more to such art than popular instruction. Similarly, although Byzantium did not, as Jaroslav Pelikan made clear, 'regard it as important or even interesting to know by whom or when an icon was crafted ... it was part of tradition',[2] the end product, affirming the inseparability of image and idea, was necessarily at the centre and not the periphery of theological debate. Indeed with one side denouncing icons as nothing but 'earth, stone, wood and misapplied skill' and the other maintaining that 'the work of iconography is a divine action' it could hardly be otherwise. Again, the relationship between artist, patron and artwork involved far more than simply securing optimal didactic effectiveness ('what the book is to those who have learned to read, that the icon is to the illiterate'[3] as St John Damascene put it), or even symbolising the relationship of imperial to divine authority. It also had the efficacy of the Incarnation itself at stake. A third example can be drawn from the Gothic Middle Ages, where the complex interdependence of art and religion, of scriptural and visual tradition, of artist and ecclesiastical patron, has long been exceptionally well documented. But even here, as Michael Camille so succinctly observed, 'if in theory God was the auctor of all, in practice Gothic artisans began to infringe His copyright'. In fact the Western Church had begun to lose its hegemony over representation at least two centuries earlier when – in contrast to the Byzantine East – it gave 'visible things only a secondary order of signification, theologically speaking' and its artists 'worked without any set of rules or ecclesiastical prerogatives'. Against this background Émile Mâle's long-established model of the deferential Gothic craftsman surely seems increasingly atypical, and the Church's own sustained efforts to define and separate 'correct' visual representations from 'incorrect' idols appear – in practice at least – to have been increasingly unrealistic. A final, equally well-known, example can be drawn from sixteenth-century Colmar. Here, as Andrée Hayum has so convincingly demonstrated, although the iconography of Grünewald's great Isenheim altarpiece was still very precisely geared to the religious institution that commanded it (a monastic order devoted to the care of the sick), it was by no means simply as 'a didactic aide memoire or gentle goad to contemplation nor as a surrogate Scripture' that the artist's masterwork operated. It was also, as Hayum shows, perceived by artist and patron alike as 'a powerful and legitimate agent for spiritual transformation … a perceptual equivalent of the Presence to be witnessed by the worshipper at the Mass'.[4]

All four of these examples underline the complex agendas – credal, institutional, political, artistic and personal – that underpin the basic triangulation between religion, art and artist that has informed our discussion so far. Other case studies regularly recur throughout the history of religious art. Many are routine commissions executed by unexceptional artists in unexceptional settings, their provenance unrecorded and unexplained, their surviving documentation – if surviving at all – often no more than a brief item in an account book. Others, usually by more famous hands, and in more famous settings, have received sustained and undivided scholarly attention. Three are of especial interest to us here.

The first is Fra Angelico's decoration of the Convent of San Marco in Florence. When a branch of the Dominican Order took over the convent from the Silvestrines in the 1430s, they were seeking to establish stricter observance to the Rule of St

Dominic than customary at the local mother church of Santa Maria Novella. A lay supporter of the 'Observance' (as the reformist group were called) was the very rich and politically influential banker Cosimo de' Medici, and it was he who paid for the extensive structural modifications to the convent, and eventually became its leading 'converse', or lay brother. It was here, between 1438 and about 1452, that a local friar of the Order, and formerly a painter, Giovanni di Fiesole (known posthumously as Fra Angelico), created over fifty frescos in the monastic cells and communal spaces. When completed, the outcome constituted what has been called 'the most extensive programme of convent decoration ever carried out'. It is also one of the acknowledged masterpieces of fifteenth-century Florentine art.

These are the basic facts. Behind them lies the now familiar triangulation of religion, art and artist. In Fra Angelico's case the triangle is tightly interlocking. For not merely was he that rarity in Renaissance art, an artist who was exclusively a religious painter (no secular works are known), but he was also, equally rarely, a religious professional as well as an artistic one. Indeed as William Hood, the leading authority on San Marco, remarks, 'it is sometimes difficult to distinguish between Fra Angelico's professional services to the Dominicans and those he owed it by virtue of obedience'.[5] Both converged in a 'brief' which seems to have been bureaucratically and personally assigned, although the documentary evidence is slender. Retrospectively this had three components. One was to use art, whether conventual frescoes or altarpieces, to help secure and reinforce the order's traditionally corporate, if periodically fissile, identity. The second, not unrelated to the first, was to use, as Hood describes it, 'three favourite Dominican visual ideas to unite all the disparate parts of the decoration as a conceptual ensemble – the order's history expressed through commemorative portraits of its most prominent members, the role of exemplars, and especially St Dominic's manners of praying, and finally the use of images as emblems of the liturgy set down in the order's formal 'Constitutions'. Such images (as much as words) were to help form prayerfulness in an institutional setting'[6] (*Figure 8*).

Hood gives a detailed, and fascinating, account of the function of images in what he calls the 'ritual topography' of the monastic enclosure, and emphasises the didactic intent behind them. Distinct messages, visually coded, were directed at distinct groups within the monastic community – the preaching friars, the novices still in formation, and the lay brothers whose work was restricted to the cloister. Fra Angelico, as both artist and long-serving Dominican (he had served as prior, subprior and syndic out in Fiesole), was clearly aware of his key role in transmitting, pictorially, the basic ideals of monastic spirituality from one generation of friars to the next, and how his images were being used programmatically to shape the religious imagination of those 'professionals' whose task it was to preach to the laity. In this sense what Hood calls his 'experiential familiarity' with Dominican theology was a major factor in Fra Angelico's work as both friar and artist. Yet while maybe subordinating his artistic development to his religious vocation, it may also have enabled him – in the San Marco context at least – to articulate and communicate certain religious ideas and practices in a pictorial language of exceptional originality and power, albeit largely within the confines of his own order.

The second case study occurs almost exactly five hundred years after the first. It, too, has a Dominican subtext (although more by accident than design) and the basic triangulation of religion, art and artist is again discernable. But there the resemblances end. Here we are encountering an internationally known artist, Henri Matisse, then in his early eighties, who undertook the design of an entire chapel – the building, stained glass, murals, crucifix, altar, pews, confessional door and vestments. 'I consider it', he said before its consecration in 1951 (which he was too frail to attend), 'in spite of its imperfections, to be my masterpiece.'[7] Those familiar with Matisse's entire œuvre, and especially his paintings, may choose to differ, but his Chapelle du Rosaire at Vence (*Figure 9*) – the only decorative commission ever offered to him in France – is nonetheless a religious artwork of outstanding quality.

The sources of the commission are to be found neither within the higher echelons of the French Catholic Church nor among a wealthy local rural or urban mercantile elite – especially in the aftermath of the Second World War. Its provenance is more like the plot of a conventionally religiose nineteenth-century novella. In 1947 Matisse was approached, unexpectedly, by a Dominican novice, Sister Jacques-Marie, who was working in the Foyer Lacordaire, a conventual rest home for tubercular girls opposite his own villa in Vence. He knew her already as Monique Bourgeois, who had been his nurse – and studio assistant – during his long convalescence from the duodenal cancer that so nearly killed him in 1941. This time she brought him a watercolour design for a stained-glass window in the convent's proposed new oratory. Matisse's immediate response was to offer to design the entire project himself, and to pay a substantial portion of the costs involved. His motives were mixed – affection for the former Monique (who had occasionally sat for him, according to Françoise Gilot), and a desire to counter the latest well-publicised exhibition of large canvasses by his friend and rival Picasso at the Maison de la Pensée Française in Paris. Above all, perhaps, the feeling, already expressed in a letter to his daughter Marguerite in February 1945, that

> painting seems to be finished for me now.... I'm for decoration. There I give everything I can – I put into it all the acquisitions of my life. In pictures, I can only go back over the same ground … but in design and decoration, I have the mastery, I'm sure of it.[8]

What is conspicuously absent from these already mixed motives is any hint of an overtly religious one on Matisse's part, or any evidence that he saw the Vence project as either a thanks offering for his escape from potentially fatal illness a few years before or as a long-postponed journey back to the Catholicism of his childhood. What emerges instead is something less predictable and more complex still. Part of it surfaced when Picasso – whose aggressive anti-clerical, anti-religious stance was powerfully shaped by his Spanish Civil War experiences – expressed his dismay at his friend undertaking a religious project at all ('he's whoring' he wrote to Matisse's studio assistant

Lydia Delectorskaya). 'Pablo asked Matisse if he had become a believer', Françoise Gilot recalls.

> Matisse answered that the chapel was giving him the opportunity to work on all the different aspects of a complete environment and that for him it was an artistic project. 'But do you pray?' Matisse answered: 'No, not really; I meditate. Always aiming towards serenity. I would say that I am closer to Buddhism than to anything else.'[9]

The other identifiable input came, more predictably, from Père Couturier, closely identified with the 'L'Art Sacrée' movement within post-war French Catholicism, and who, as the leading Dominican authority on contemporary art, discussed Matisse's chapel project with him almost from its conception.[10] Their relationship was close, if also reserved, to judge from the published sources. Couturier, who knew many leading French and international artists personally – Assy alone is extraordinary testimony to this – admired Matisse especially for his 'absolute sincerity' and for his 'incomparable instinct for the plastic mediums and their spiritual power'. Matisse, in his turn, not only liked the tall, austere, yet worldly and outgoing monk, who posed in person for the first studies of the St Dominic altar decorations at Vence and Assy. He also agreed with Couturier's oft-repeated belief that regardless of artists' conscious political choices and philosophical opinions, the act of painting was a religious act when truly inspired. 'We do not ask the artist to be a believer', the latter told Picasso in Matisse's presence – an outlook reassuringly consonant with Matisse's own rather tenuous religious affiliations. Indeed, until the 1940s, he had entirely avoided religious subjects altogether, and as late as a year before undertaking the chapel at Vence he still considered such themes alien to his creative spirit. As William Rubin comments, 'during his long career, he had never evinced particular interest in Catholicism, and his few references to "God" and "religion" were vague allusions to the mystery of creation'.[11] For example, in *Notes of a Painter* (1908), Matisse could write of preferring the human figure to landscape as a vehicle 'for the so-to-say religious feeling that I have towards life'. Nearly forty years later, in *Jazz*, he famously answered a rhetorical question about belief in God by saying 'When I work … I feel somehow aided by someone who makes me do things that are beyond me.'[12] Such a stance seems rather at odds with his equally strong sense, reiterated in several letters to Couturier, of the need to safeguard his own independence of mind throughout every stage of the four-year Vence project. Couturier frequently reassured him on this issue.

Even then there could be difficulties. For example, when asked by Brother Rayssiguier (a young Dominican ex-architect closely involved with the chapel plan from the beginning) to try a religious subject – 'a Virgin for example' – Matisse replied: 'No, I do not feel such subjects … when I paint something profane, God directs me, and it goes beyond me. If I tried to make a Virgin, I would be forcing things. God would leave me to myself.'[13] Unsurprisingly, perhaps, it was only a matter of months before some of his plans for the chapel ('the work of my entire lifetime') were challenged by Rayssiguier himself. 'Do not yield an inch on Christian atmosphere', the latter reminded him, 'but retain as much Matisse as possible.' He suspected, however, that 'the inch will be difficult to measure' – and he was entirely correct. The differences between priest and artist soon exploded in a 'letter full of reproaches and complaints' sent to Matisse by Rayssiguier, and Couturier was called in to mediate. Although the latter wrote that 'what [Matisse] pictures is very different from what [Rayssiguier] pictured, and is much better', it was Matisse who finally, in this particular instance, abandoned his first window designs for the nave and got to work on a second, while also confessing, rather truculently, to Couturier, 'I don't regret it though – for I know why my first design was the right one, the best one.'

Given such complex and conflicting cross-currents – personal, institutional, aesthetic and credal – Matisse's Chapel itself is an exceptionally coherent tour de force. Most art-historical accounts of it pay especial attention to the simplicity of the design (consonant with the Dominican order's own aesthetic), the subtle fenestration (with very tall windows creating intense, highly charged, luminosity), the contrasting use of black outlines on a white-tiled ground for figurative imagery (especially for the minimalist 'Stations of the Cross') and the artist's sole responsibility not merely for the chapel's form and decoration, but for all the fittings, and even the brilliantly coloured vestments. More relevant in the context of this book is the precise relationship between the evolution of the Chapel over four years, and Matisse's own interior life during that period. In one sense certain inner contradictions emerge. 'I did not feel the need to convert in order to do the chapel', he told André Legard in

1951, 'My interior attitude has not altered; it has remained the same as it was when I was confronted by a face, a chair, or a bowl of fruit.'[14] Yet in the same year 'Matisse could say, in his introduction to a picture book celebrating the completion of the Chapel, 'This is not a work that I chose, but rather a work for which I was chosen by fate',[15] having already reflected to Couturier a year earlier, 'From a certain moment on it isn't me any more, it's a revelation; all I have to do is give myself.'[16]

With the 'Stations of the Cross', Matisse moved from broadly metaphysical experience to something more overtly religious, even confessional, in his approach. For although he links medium to message quite explicitly ('the ceramic tiles are the spiritual essential and explain the meaning of the monument') the message itself created mixed and powerful emotions in the artist. One was that, as he told Picasso (to whom he went for advice). it enforced a 'rare and unwilling' recognition of the existence of pain and suffering, which he was unsure he could depict. Another was that it forced him back to his own store of Christian imagery. As Couturier was to recall, 'speaking of his Way of the Cross, he [Matisse] told us "Things like that, you have to know them by heart so well that you could draw them blindfold."'[17] Which he did, not blindfold, but painstakingly, and making hundreds of sketches. The third emotion was what Matisse himself described as 'tempestuous'. It is worth quoting him in full.

> To depict the Stations, marked 'the encounter of the artist
> with the great tragedy of Christ, which makes the impassioned
> spirit of the artist flow out over the chapel.'[18] Initially, having

conceived it in the same spirit as that of the first two panels [St Dominic and the Virgin and Child], he made it a procession of succeeding scenes. But finding himself gripped by the pathos of so profound a tragedy, he upset the order of his composition. The artist quite naturally became its principal actor; instead of reflecting the tragedy, he has experienced it and this is how he has expressed it.

In other words, the artist's own experience of the episode shapes his depiction of it. The result is that the Stations are not in the traditional spacing along the wall but as one composition in which the eye rather than the body does the moving. One modern commentator has described their 'splintered composition and ugly, scrawling line', and Matisse himself described his figurative scheme as 'very rough; it will prompt most people who see it to despair … all this forces us to focus – forces our gaze to stop at each station'.[19]

In sum, it would be easy to conclude that Matisse mainly saw his Vence project as what Rubin has described as 'a testimony to friendship and charity rather than religious faith',[20] but also one with serious religious purposes – 'the creation of religious space.… I want those who will come into my chapel to feel purified and relieved of their burdens.'[21] Yet it is not difficult to identify a more explicitly Christian subtext, especially in his deeply felt account of the 'Stations'. This is also the professed agnostic who could not only confess to Couturier ('my friend and confidant') that 'I am inhabited by things that waken me but do not reveal themselves',[22] but also tell his anti-Christian friend and rival Pablo Picasso that 'I'm not a believer, but when things are going badly, I say my childhood, my first communion, prayers over again, and this brings me back to a world where things are better.'[23] This does not, of course, make Matisse a 'Christian' artist, but his prolonged engagement with the Vence project not only places him firmly within our religion–art–artist triangulation. It also served to crystallise his personal religious identity, if not his faith. As Françoise Gilot, who knew him well at the time, so perceptively concluded: 'Matisse was caught in an ascending spiral of vision. He became more deeply involved than he thought he would, for spiritual, if not religious reasons.'[24]

Our third, and final, example involves the same essential triangulation – between artist, artwork and religion – as at Fra Angelico's San Marco and Matisse's Vence Chapel, but at a more psychologically and theologically complex level, and with a more radical aesthetic outcome, than either.[25] The basic story of the so-called Rothko Chapel is well known. In 1965, John and Dominique de Menil, a very wealthy, French-born, Texan couple with a strong interest in contemporary art and especially Abstract Expressionism, approached Mark Rothko (with whose work they were already familiar – indeed they had bought their first Rothko back in 1957) with an invitation to collaborate with the rising young architect Philip Johnson on a campus chapel (to be explicitly designed around Rothko's paintings) at St Thomas University, Houston, Texas. However, the Basilean Fathers, whose university it was, had more traditional expectations of the chapel than the de Menils (their main benefactors), tensions arose, and the chapel itself was resited at nearby Rice University, and placed under the control of an ecumenical body. Before long, Rothko and Johnson too were at loggerheads, principally over the way the space would be lit. When the de Menils sided with the artist, Johnson withdrew from the project, and the building was completed by two local Houston architects, who adhered closely to Rothko's own expectations. Back in New York, Rothko worked on the canvases in a newly rented studio, a former riding school. Eventually eighteen canvases were sent to Houston, of which fourteen were hung in the octagonal space. The chapel was dedicated on 27 February 1971. Although Rothko had been intimately involved in the process of planning and building, he never visited Houston in person, and never saw the finished installation. Two days before the dedication, on 25 February, in New York, at the age of 66, he had committed suicide.

Beneath the bare facts and tragic symmetry lie several very powerful personal subtexts. Most evident, perhaps, was the immediate physical and cultural context of the commission itself. We know not only that as a younger painter he had been moved by Fra Angelico's frescoes in the convent of San Marco, but also that the Houston project itself reminded him (as perhaps the de Menils, and their mentor, Père Couturier, intended that it should) of Matisse's own chapel at Vence. Indeed Rothko's oft-quoted letter to the de Menils (soon after he had begun work on their commission), where he talks of 'the magnitude, on every level of experience and meaning, of the task in which you have involved me, exceeds all my preconceptions. And it is teaching me to extend myself beyond what I thought was possible for me',[26] carries echoes of Matisse's own strong sense of Vence as 'the work of my entire lifetime'. The proposed location, too, appealed to Rothko's long-held belief (very different from Matisse) that his paintings should be seen in an isolated environment, away from other distractions and other art – a kind of sanctuary where they might perform what is essentially a sacramental function. At Houston, his silent, elevated paintings could receive their proper regard (quiet contemplation) and their proper recognition (as sacred objects) without migrating through the hands of a series of dealers and collectors, and ending up in a museum setting. Any journey there, too, should have serious intent. As Jonathan Ahearn, one of his studio assistants at the time, later recalled: 'you had to make a pilgrimage to see his icons … it was very important to him that you make an effort to see them, that they not be just accessible. These were religious experiences which you had to bring yourself to.'[27] Such experiences would, in Rothko's view, be optimised in the octagonal ground plan he finally persuaded Johnson to adopt. Here, although he undoubtedly admired, and vividly recalled, the octagonal Byzantine church of Santa Maria Assunta on Torcello, he was largely motivated by purely aesthetic rather than any religious considerations. Here, Dominique de Menil's own account of Rothko's tactics is especially revealing. 'Afraid', she recalled, 'that the octagonal shape might be rejected, he sought to justify it by looking for precedents. He went so far as pretending [to me] that he has spoken to Meyer Shapiro [the distinguished art historian] and learned from him that indeed such central plans had been used in early Christian times.'[28] In reality, of course, his primary criterion was the way the plan would serve his murals: the choice of the octagon (although liturgically aligned to newly recommended Vatican II practice) was well suited to frontality and symmetry, both of which are salient characteristics of the paintings themselves.

For Rothko, even such relatively prosaic features of the chapel as its location, function and ground plan were, like the interior lighting scheme (itself a specific bone of contention with Philip Johnson), a far from prosaic matter. This was not merely due to a recurrent need to, in his phrase, 'control the situation' as far as sites for the public display of his own creativity were concerned, or to his periodic bouts of irascibility and depression. It was also because he saw both the chapel setting, even in a studio mock-up, and his paintings for it – the latter endlessly contemplated, worked on, modified – as the supreme opportunity to express what Georgine Oeri has called 'his fundamental premise: the confidence in the naturalness of the spirit and in the possibility of it being manifest'.[29] Here, as in so much of his later work, the physical and the metaphysical converge. 'What is wonderful about Mark', the critic Dore Ashton wrote in her journal on 7 July 1964 (after discussing his new chapel commission with him), 'is that he aspires, and is still capable of believing that his work can have some purpose – spiritual if you like – that is not sullied by the world.'[30] In practice, of course, such a controlling vision, if not exactly 'sullied by the world', was supplemented by other, more identifiable inputs – his Jewish upbringing, his intense early exposure to Dostoevsky, Kierkegaard and, above all, Nietzsche, and his reawakened interest in the early patristic writers, especially Origen. The latter's threefold approach to the scriptures – literal, ethical and allegorical – seemed, to

Rothko, wholly consonant with his own personal and artistic trajectory, with the chapel, perhaps, as the ultimate spiritual allegory. Above all, he was, in Ashton's phrase, the 'natural heritor'[31] of Pascal's Deus absconditus (itself, of course, a Jewish as well as a Christian concept), refracted further through the nineteenth century's intellectual conflicts between faith and doubt, and then investing Rothko (in common with many other twentieth-century artists) with the power to illuminate and inspire, yet unable, like his predecessors, to assume the presence of a prime mover. Yet while Rothko would either deny the religious character imputed to his paintings by others ('he hated that kind of talk' one studio assistant recalled[32]), or deliberately demystify his own religious perspective ('the people who weep before my pictures are having the same religious experience I had when I painted them'[33]), his mature work is surely one of the great spiritual realisations of twentieth-century art in any medium. His patron Dominique de Menil was surely right when she wrote that Rothko's 'chapel venture, which conjured his heart, his soul, and his total energies, evokes the pursuit of mystics, entering into silent darkness. It is beyond the support of words and images that God can be approached.'[34]

Yet both the form and content of the Houston Chapel (*Figure 10*) also carry distinguishable 'religious' as well as 'spiritual' resonances. We know, for example, that Rothko saw the octagonal ground plan not merely in historicist, Byzantine–Christian terms, nor just as 'the truly controlled situation' he had always demanded, but also as a place where 'East and West merge' – ecumenical sentiments only actualised after his death. At the same time, during the three years he worked on the project, he clearly believed that his murals would be hung in a Catholic chapel – a religious environment modelled, quite consciously in his patrons' minds at least, on the Chapelle du Rosaire at Vence. Rothko had, in any case, already painted a neo-Byzantine 'Last Supper', 'Crucifixion' and 'Gethsemane' in the late 1930s and, as is clear from his recently rediscovered and newly published manuscript *The Artist's Reality*,[35] written in 1940–41, he had also fully absorbed Christian themes and Christian iconography in some art-historical detail. But from the late 1950s onwards, he was moving towards a kind of transcendental abstraction ('I want to paint both the finite and infinite') and his paintings themselves are very precise in their refusal to entertain traditional narratives or even images, or to allow vague religiosity to mar their immediacy. Indeed when the critic Brian O'Doherty visited Rothko at work on the chapel murals, the latter remarked at one point that 'he could have fulfilled the commission with blank canvases "and made it work"'.[36]

Yet at the same time any visual encounter with Rothko's large, dark, minimalistic Houston canvases is shaped by a much more standardised set of Christian iconography than we might first imagine or allow. If the chapel is, as already suggested, decidedly Christian in its octagonal arrangement, echoing a traditional baptistery design, the paintings on its walls also hint at a similar provenance. The two axial murals at the entrance and in the apse are as dialectically opposed as the mosaics of the Last Judgement and the celestial vision of the Virgin and Child at Torcello. Here Rothko creates the same tension, where a hanging black field, like an impending doom, at the entrance, is cancelled out by the central panel of the apse, painted in a warmer tone – a more vibrant purple. On the facing walls, between four relatively monochrome canvases, are two other triptychs each with a central panel raised, carrying with it a faint visual echo of Renaissance crucifixions. Yet while further readings in terms of Christian iconography are inevitably imprecise, there is a completeness about the whole ensemble – the alternating triptychs, the dramatic single entrance canvas, the four almost monochrome pauses, the comparative brightness of the centrepiece, the richness of tone and colour achieved within a single sombre mood, and indeed the variety of moods accessible within it – which resonates strongly with earlier Christian responses to sacred space, while in no sense replicating them.

At the same time, unlike Matisse at Vence, Rothko's chapel images are, as it were, supra-pictorial, perhaps even supra-Christian. Indeed his fellow artist Robert Motherwell (following a studio visit early in 1967) quoted Rothko as saying that in the beginning he had thought of them as pictures. 'But then, he considered that people praying would not want to be distracted by pictures. They wanted an ambience.'[37] This visitors certainly continue to experience, to judge from remarks to be found in successive guest books such as 'a sacred feeling filled me and inspired peace and awe' or 'at a time of turmoil and change [it was] a peaceful contemplative respite' or 'we let the space invite us to meditation; we do not meditate because we have been told that is what one does when confronted with a triptych or a baptistry'.[38]

Yet the ultimate impact of Rothko's chapel also lies in the overwhelming poignancy of the artist's attempt to forge, or re-fashion – for him and for us – some sensory connection with the transcendent realm. When we look at his Houston paintings *in situ*, we are also virtually forced to look beyond them. We are urged, to adapt Jack Flam's memorable description, 'to give ourselves over to some sort of mystical experience: to be enveloped in a contemplative trance in which the paint surface seems to throb with a kind of metaphysical energy'.[39] Whether, in our own time, we are still able to apprehend this larger dimension, which Rothko rarely sought to define, but only to make visible and felt, remains problematic for painter and public alike. As Mark Rothko himself, with extraordinary prescience, remarked to a fellow artist a few months before his own death, 'the struggle is beyond painting, not with painting'.[40] This is an issue to which we shall return.

7

artists as 'believers'

The preceding chapter explored, in some detail, the relation-ship of certain artists to certain religious institutions. Here we examine a partially reverse process: the role of religious identity, ideas, and personal beliefs in shaping artistic self-expression.

In the past, as we have seen, both processes were usually visible, interdependent and culturally acknowledged. Indeed in this sense it is virtually impossible to separate the history of religious art from the history of religion itself – a proposition which holds good across the major religious traditions, as well as among their 'archaic' precursors and today's less developed societies. Within Christianity it is a relatively straightforward exercise to single out individuals in whose work both processes self-evidently converge. Within the Eastern Orthodox tradition, for example, icons were, and still largely are, painted by priests, whose work is unsigned. Indeed the reconvened Second Council of Nicaea (787 AD) specifically stated that 'icon painting was not invented by painters; it is, on the contrary, an established institution and tradition of the church' and that 'icons are in painting what the Holy Scriptures are in writing: an aesthetic form of the truth, which is beyond the understanding of Man and cannot be comprehended by the senses.'[1] Hence before setting to work the icon painter purifies himself by fasting, prayer, confession and communion, and his technique is itself rigidly circumscribed throughout. Typically, he takes a small panel of birch, pine, lime or cypress wood, smooths a planed area, leaving a border which forms a natural frame separating the image from the outside world. Two slats of wood, placed behind, prevent warping. The painter then sticks a thin piece of tissue over the planed surface and covers it with a layer of gesso to fix the natural colours, which can be ground with holy water and saints' relics. He then varnishes the painted image with boiled linseed oil, which heightens the colours for a while, then slowly dulls them. The finished icon is then to be blessed. This technique, although paraphrased from a twentieth-century manual,[2] is virtually identical to that first formally set down in the early tenth century.

Although there are some identifiable stylistic changes in icon painting (notably through Italian Renaissance compositions in-fluencing Greek pictorial traditions), it remains extraordinary that while Italy was responding to the advent of realism in its various forms, such as linear and aerial perspective, Ger-many and the Netherlands were nurturing highly individu-alistic interpreters of religious themes (Dürer, Memling, van der Weyden), and Rembrandt's chiaroscuro (in both oil and etching) was transforming the pictorial depiction of Biblical narrative, Eastern Orthodox icon painters should have continued to produce the self-same figures, in the same style, acting out the same unvarying visual theology. Very occasionally a brilliant maverick would step beyond the Orthodox Byzantine canon. One was Theophanes the Greek,[3] an icon and fresco painter who went to Russia in the 1370s, and whose use of a sketchy 'impressionistic' technique (with sweeping brush strokes, bold colours and vivid highlighting – derived ultimately from Late Antique wall paintings) was the product not of icon manuals and established theological orthodoxies, but, as he confessed, of his own religious imagination. Another was his younger contemporary and intermittent assistant Andrei Rublev,[4] who was a monk, based at the Andronikov monastery in Moscow, from 1400 until his death in 1430. His work, although not pro-lific, is ground-breaking art-historically – breaking away from the angular severities of Greek iconic tradition towards new harmony and beauty. His colours are shimmering and opalescent pinks, lapis lazulis and pale golds, their transparency giving the impression of being illuminated from within by a light from another world. His physical forms are rounded, and their facial expressions are at once austere and compassionate. His output is also ground-breaking theologically, and no more so than in his 'Old Testament Trinity'[5] (*Figure 11*), now in the Tretyakov Gallery in Moscow.

The early Fathers of the Church saw the incident described in Genesis 18 as a foreshadowing of the later revelation of the Holy Trinity. The Lord appears to Abraham by the oak of

Mamre, and Abraham sees three men, to whom he gives hospitality. The 'hospitality of Abraham' is seen as a meeting of God and Abraham, and by the late fourth century the theme is found in wall paintings and soon becomes a common theme in Christian art. For about a thousand years thereafter the visual representation of this theme included the three visitors shown as winged beings to signify their heavenly nature, the figures of Abraham and Sarah, and sometimes a servant killing a calf, and other illustrative details. Rublev recasts this iconography quite radically, by drastically reducing the details traditionally associated with this theme, and concentrates instead on the figures of the three angels. Abraham, Sarah, servants and other details are removed; the home of Abraham and Sarah and the oak of Mamre are reduced to symbols alongside the very distorted mountain peak, and the focus of attention is now the three angels grouped around the table, with the chalice of sacrifice in the centre. Rublev's whole composition is assembled round an unseen circle – the shape of the mandorla often used to represent the divine source of the particular revelation given in icons of the Transfiguration of Christ and the Dormition of the Virgin. What is novel here, both theologically and aesthetically, is the way unity and diversity are held together so vividly in Rublev's composition, representing both the perfection of communion and mutual love within the Holy Trinity, and also the mutual involvement of each person of the Trinity in the work of revelation and redemption. Interestingly, the painting, itself a work of then unprecedented pictorial invention, not only shows the artist as a source of theological innovation in his own time, but also, 140 years later, prompted a Church Council to proclaim his style as the true standard of artistic orthodoxy 'to be followed in all perpetuity'.

Nurtured within the same Orthodox tradition, but rapidly transcending it, both aesthetically and visually, is El Greco.[6] Growing up in Crete in the third quarter of the sixteenth century, where his birthplace Heraklion (then under Venetian rule) housed a number of ateliers, headed by gifted artists (El Greco among them) who were engaged in what might almost be described as the mass production of icons for export and for the domestic market. The result was a hybrid art of considerable technical excellence, ranging from Orthodox icon painting to devotional artworks far closer to Venetian Catholic humanism. Although the icon, in whatever genre, still retained its function in Orthodox worship, its continuing theological as well as stylistic constraints (and perhaps his own professional ambitions) clearly prompted El Greco to emigrate to the West, and 'retool' himself within a less Orthodox, and more overtly Catholic, cultural tradition. Although this process occurred initially in Venice and Rome, and involved apprenticeships with Titian and Tintoretto, it was in Spain, and especially at Toledo (where he remained for the rest of his life), that El Greco's religious outlook and its artistic expression (already nurtured in the most purely religious painting tradition that has ever existed) really begin to converge. It is not simply that, on the evidence of his altarpieces alone, we can detect a fusion of visual and religious intensity. It is also that, as has been well documented, he had a well-developed habit of personal devotion, focused and deepened by the influence of the Counter-Reformation in general, and Ignatian spirituality in particular. The practice of the Spiritual Exercises (no doubt more pervasive among his patrons than his fellow-artists!) encouraged an immediacy of experience and a mental participation in the events and details of the sufferings of Christ's Passion, which clearly quickened his artistic imagination and imparted to his work even more intense religious feeling. Indeed El Greco's pictorial emphasis on physical actuality – appealing directly to the senses – closely mirror's those passages of the Exercises which suggest that emotional engagement can lead to the spiritual domain. Sometimes the combination was too much for his ecclesiastical patrons. For example, the 'Disrobing of Christ' (*Figure 12*) was rejected by the Toledo Cathedral Chapter, who complained that Christ was being represented disrespectfully by being surrounded by his executioners in such a way that some of them stood higher in the picture than he did. El Greco sued the Chapter for his fee, and although the assessors unanimously praised the picture and supported his claim, the episode is indicative of the potential tensions inherent between a theologically flexible artist and a theologically conservative church body. At the same time it seems almost self-evident that El Greco not only saw much of his art as functioning in the service of Christian truth, but also as communicating – unequivocally – the almost mystical intensity of his own religious convictions.

A generation later than El Greco, and embedded within a profoundly different religious tradition, is Rembrandt van Rijn (1606–69).[7] The child of Protestant Reformed Church parents,

Rembrandt was baptised, and later married, within the same, essentially Calvinist, tradition. And while El Greco was, like Rembrandt's contemporary Rubens, working in a courtly, aristocratic and Catholic milieu, Rembrandt's own world was largely an urban, commercial, middle-class and Protestant one, without any strongly developed tradition of patronage for religious subject matter. It is unsurprising, therefore, that in only one instance do we know of any work of his specifically intended for a liturgical setting – the series on the Passion commissioned in the 1630s for Prince Frederick Henry, the Dutch Stadtholder, and probably for his private chapel. The five paintings, now in Munich, belong to the early phase of the artist's career, and reflect both his indebtedness to traditional Baroque motifs and his simultaneous unease with them. Yet by the end of his life Rembrandt had etched, drawn or painted about eight hundred and fifty religious works, nearly all on biblical subjects.

The explanations for this marked disparity between a very restricted market for religious art among Protestants and Rembrandt's own productivity in the genre are relatively complex. On the 'demand' side it could be argued that a majority of the wealthier Dutch Protestants (although enthusiastic about portraits or domestic scenes) either shared the prevailing aniconic aesthetic of Calvinism or, ironically enough, preferred the sensuous appeal of the Catholic Baroque on their own walls. On the 'supply' side, Rembrandt was a master of both paintings and etchings. Since etchings could be sold more easily for the home and the public market, whereas a painting needed a patron, he gave considerable time to his etchings. Furthermore, he was well aware that etchings were particularly suited to those Protestants who wanted to have works of art in their homes relatively inexpensively, and for whom private meditation in front of them was quite acceptable, whereas their liturgical use in churches was not, partly because of their Catholic subject matter, and partly because public services were not liturgical in character.

Yet there is far more to Rembrandt's choice of the primary genre for his religious art than mere entrepreneurial sleight of hand. For one thing, although his educational background had not sensitised him to the subtler nuances of Protestant theological discourse, his artistic style (in whatever medium) and Reform mindset form a coherent whole: style and content are matched. But it was not a liturgical art or one created for a church setting. It was rather a meditative art, one that centred on the individual consciousness, on the states of the soul in themselves and then on their relation or non-relation to others. Its emphasis, in any case, was on the difference that grace makes in specific situations – a mirror of the Gospel message. It had little to do with human community, except the community of sinners or humanity in its problems As Visser 't Hooft (himself a distinguished twentieth-century Dutch Protestant) puts it, 'Rembrandt was the painter of the grace of God, exhibited to the unworthy, the unimportant, those without merit, in such a way that only the grace of god mattered.'[8]

Although there are other identifiable components to Rembrandt's religious formation – his associations and friendships with Mennonites, his sympathetic acquaintance with the Jewish community, his links, in later life, with an informal

Calvinist cell devoted to Christian meditation and poetry – and its aesthetic expression – one other powerful feature is crucial to our understanding of both. To cite Visser 't Hooft again, 'Rembrandt's Christianity cannot be defined in terms of the Church, but is the result of his personal encounter with the Bible.'[9] We know that his mother read the Scriptures to him as a boy, that his fellow-students at the Latin school in Leiden read the Bible daily, and that as an adult he was nourished by his reading of the Bible, which was relatively free of the theological assumptions of the conservatives and liberals of his time. All this reinforced both his religious and his artistic identity, reflected not only in the extraordinary self-portrait now at Kenwood, where he portrays himself as a successor to Giotto (complete with perfect circles behind him!) but in the overwhelming proportion of biblical themes in his entire output.

These not only document Rembrandt's uncomplicated piety, and testify to his intimate knowledge of Bible stories. They also demonstrate how his religious outlook transformed the Baroque aesthetic of his early years and brought about a transition from the melodramatic effects and actions displayed in bodily postures and contours to the depiction of God's presence in the inner psychic states of composed, relatively inactive individuals. It is as if the action emanated from the countenance of a single figure, as in the Christ figure, or from countenance to countenance without dramatic action. Furthermore the depiction of humans has changed from idealised figures to identifiable human beings in their unique, ordinary lives. Rembrandt's paintings, and especially the etchings, reflect the concern of the Calvinist

Reformers with the personal relationship between an individual and God, and also with the knowledge of God which is found in the common task, daily work, and family relationships. The Christ figure himself is depicted as a servant, the Son of God become Man. Rembrandt often focuses on the humanity of Christ, but, as Christopher Joby has argued, very persuasively, 'he uses his craftsmanship to suggest also the transcendental nature of Christ, and he tries, as far as is possible on a two-dimensional plane, to represent both the human and the divine natures of Christ'.[10] This was, in direct contravention of Calvin's prohibition of the depiction of Christ in art – on the grounds that it would only show one of his two natures. However, there are many instances in Rembrandt's work of the artist deliberately creating the effect of a light emanating from Christ (*Figure 13*), and in these deeply felt exercises in visual Christology we are invariably presented with a Christ very much of this world, but also, through the use of light, a Christ whose divine nature is equally clear.

This preoccupation with depicting the corporeal yet transcendent nature of Christ, especially in a world where some scholars were beginning to challenge both his historicity and his divinity, was central to the Pre-Raphaelite painter William Holman Hunt.[11] Although the Pre-Raphaelites' writings contain remarkably few references to any explicitly religious imperatives behind their overtly religious paintings, and most of the Brotherhood disclaimed any formal affiliation with any religious group, especially High Church Anglicanism, Holman Hunt is a clear, and self-proclaimed, exception. Indeed his capacity for personal religious reflection was, even by mid-Victorian standards, prodigious, and probably greater than that of any painter of religious subject matter in any period. 'You know', he wrote to his fellow-Pre-Raphaelite William Bell Scott from Jerusalem in 1870,

> how above all my life's affections is my love of Christ ... since leaving England I have been reading Seeley's 'Ecce Homo', Renan's 'Life of Christ', etc ... also I have further re-read very attentively the whole Testament, marking down all its questionable points ... the result is that I believe more defiantly than ever ... that Christianity, even in its highest pretensions, must be true. I do not use the phrase in relation to the authority of the Church. I mean the direct supernatural origin and nature of Christ, that he really came down from heaven, from the dwelling place of the divinity, that he performed miracles ... my belief is that as man was a new development in animal life, so was Christ to us.[12]

In its Victorian context such Christocentrism almost defies a clear-cut label, for it transcends unreconstructed evangelicalism on the one hand and Tractarianism on the other, and is, if anything, closer to the Broad Church position ('a party to end parties in the Church') than either. In practice Hunt had long and continuing associations with members of all three religious groups, although, as George Landow has convincingly argued, his treatment of religious themes, with its emphasis on strict morality, personal conversion, typology, and a literalist interpretation of the Bible, point more in an evangelical direction than any other. But more important in the context of this chapter is Hunt's continual agonising over whether his own art 'could serve effectively as an auxiliary of the Protestant religion', or ever attain 'real religious feeling'. He was also deeply dispirited by what he called 'the de-mystified sacred art' of so many of his contemporaries, where 'the pictures at their best are only quaint antiquated patterns. They have no relation to the living minds of men', and are 'destructive in their impact upon the church goer in whose mind the galvanized puppets portrayed are calculated to originate the idea that the story on which religion is founded is a mere myth.'[13]

Hunt's aesthetic response was more focused and intense than that of any other members of the Brotherhood, and involved two essentially interlocking strategies. One was a thoroughgoing commitment to physical and emotional realism, which was acted out in several extended visits to the Middle East. These were not only undertaken in order to apply Pre-Raphaelite principles of truth to nature to scriptural subjects, but also, as Hunt told his fellow artist Augustus Egg before his departure in January 1854, because 'my desire is very strong to make more tangible Jesus Christ's history and teaching.'[14] The area had not vastly changed since biblical times, and Hunt therefore felt that by studying the terrain and its inhabitants he could create a sacred art relevant to his own age. Although his painting 'The Scape-goat', mainly painted over twelve days by the shores of the Dead Sea, in searing heat, bitten by sandflies, and with a rifle over his knee to warn off brigands, is perhaps Hunt's best-known, if least effective, example of this quest for realism, 'The Finding of the Saviour in the Temple' – started in Jerusalem at the same time – involved an even more sustained search for verisimilitude.

In Jerusalem he studied sources in the Old and New Testaments and the Talmud, and tried, not always successfully, to persuade local Jews to sit for him. On returning to England, he obtained further models from London's Jewish community, and used the Alhambra Court at the Crystal Palace as the basis for the Temple itself. The final outcome, not exhibited until April 1860, was an extraordinary public success (attracting 800 to 1000 visitors a day, each paying a shilling entry fee), and subsequent sales of prints (about 15,000 all told) very high by Victorian standards. This was not only due to astute marketing by artist and dealer alike ('After eighteen months spent in Jerusalem and nearly five years study, Mr Hunt places his work before the public') or to strong critical acclaim (the *Manchester Guardian* noted: 'No picture of such extraordinary elaboration has been seen in our day.... Draperies, architecture, heads, and hands, are wrought to a point of complete imitative finish'[15]). It was also because, as Hunt had intended, its hyperrealism carried a religious resonance. It attempted, on a historical and archaeological plane, to show what the finding of the Saviour in the Temple was actually like at the time, and therefore to deepen the spectator's empathy with, and emotional engagement in, the life of Christ.

To such realism must be added Hunt's second aesthetic strategy for his religious art: his use of symbolism as well as realism. More specifically, through his reading, in Volume II of *Modern Painters* (1846), of Ruskin's very complex analysis of Tintoretto's 'Annunciation' in the Scuola di San Rocco,[16] Hunt realised that pre-figurative, or typological, symbolism could be used in painting to obtain a unique and indissoluble blend of realism *and* symbolism in a picture. Like Ruskin, Hunt too believed that a symbolism based on scriptural typology – the method of finding anticipations of Christ in Hebrew history – would produce a religious art that would simultaneously avoid the dangers of materialism inherent in realism, and the accompanying perils of mere academicism or gross sentimentality. How successfully Hunt avoided the latter three is open to question. Even Ruskin's own comment on 'The Scapegoat' was stinging: 'Mr Hunt has been blinded by his intense sentiment to the real weaknesses of the pictorial expression; and in his earnest desire to paint the Scapegoat, has forgotten to ask himself first whether he could paint a goat at all',[17] but his deployment of typological symbolism, especially for religious themes was, he felt, integral to their religious impact. Indeed as George Landow has so brilliantly documented, the practice of studying the Bible for types of the Saviour was already common in Hunt's day. Hence in the 'Finding of the Saviour in the Temple', for example, the more educated viewers, and especially those of an evangelical persuasion, would have connected the scene in the courtyard of the builders selecting the cornerstone of the Temple with the figure of Christ himself, the cornerstone of the New Dispensation. Even the painting's elaborate frame, also designed by Hunt, continues the symbolism within: for instance, on the left, the serpent of the Mosaic law is intertwined with the Cross.

In Hunt's earlier, and most famous, picture, 'The Light of the World' (*Figure 5*), painted between 1851 and 1853, the same fusion of symbolism and realism is operative, and doctrinally explicit.

It is clear that Christ's lantern – whether it be the light of truth or of Christian doctrine – provides most of the illumination. The promise of a new day, a new life once the soul awakens to Christ, and the natural light of the moon can shed some, too, but Christ himself must be the chief means by which one can see him. But perhaps the very elaborate symbolic motifs of the painting are not, in the last analysis, as significant to our understanding of Hunt's own religious outlook as two other factors. One, often overlooked by art historians, is that it was painted precisely in the aftermath of the much-publicised 1851 Religious Census.[18] This showed, incontrovertibly, that religious practice (established at below half the adult population) was as seriously threatened as religious belief itself, and the high-profile public debate about the future of both cannot have escaped Hunt. His 'Light of the World' was surely his pictorial response to it. At the same time it was also a highly personal *Confessio Fidei*, as his famous letter to William Bell Scott – written many years later, in 1883 – makes clear. 'At the time', he wrote,

> I had myself been much in want of some certainty as to whether there was indeed a Master who cared for aspirations in us.... It is a gratification to me to think that the meaning I accepted at the time, is through my effort made of active use to others, for indeed I painted the picture with what I thought, unworthy though I was, to be by divine command, and not simply as a good subject. When I found it I was reading the Bible, critically determined if I could to find out the flaws for myself, or its inspiration. I was in great anxiety on the point.... The figure of Christ standing at the door haunted me, gradually coming in more clearly defined meaning, with logical enrichments, waiting in the night – ever night – with

the dawn, with a light sheltered from the chance of extinction, in a lantern necessarily therefore, with a crown on His head bearing that also of thorns; with body robed like a priest, not of Christian time only, and in a world with signs of neglect and blindness. You will say that it was an emotional conversion, but there were other influences outside of sentiment.[19]

On this evidence who are we to disbelieve him?

8

from religion to spirituality

Most of our discussion thus far has centred on the relationship of art to religion, with a particular emphasis upon the inter-action of artists, institutions, patrons, beliefs and practices. The focus has been primarily upon the Western Christian tradition, although a similar analysis could have been applied to the other major religious traditions, including Islam, as well as to those within less developed societies worldwide. More limiting, per-haps, has been an implicit assumption that Western Christianity not only has provided, but *continues* to provide, a cultural and credal framework within which the relationship between art and religion is acted out. It is clearly the case that the twentieth century witnessed a number of major artists whose personal religious beliefs and identities are crucial in understanding their art – Chagall, Kandinsky, Malevich, Mondrian, Rouault, Bacon, Newman, Segal and Spencer, for example – and still the case that religious bodies continue to commission artworks for some of their sacred spaces and for liturgical use, and that well-qualified advisory bodies and expert individuals still exist to facilitate this process.[1] Yet today, although there are a number of excellent artists producing 'religious' art for religious institutions, such activities are, at the same time, becoming increasingly marginal – perhaps not unlike much of organised religion itself. In sum, today's artists are unlikely to be keyed into religious culture because there is no identifiable religious culture to be keyed into.

Some of the reasons for this have already been hinted at, even briefly identified, in earlier chapters. One is an increasing transition from a religious to an aesthetic validation of experience. More specifically, it is clear that from about 1750 art, rather than supporting and articulating church-based theology, began to separate itself from religious thought and institutions. 'Art', wrote Goethe in 1804, 'has consolidated its status as an independent cult, sometimes more flourishing than the churches themselves and Christian theology'.[2] Through such a process art has become a manifestation, in Tillich's phrase, of 'one form of the latent church'.[3] It comes to be treated as a source of both the prophetic and the redemptive in its own right. A second explanation is rooted in what can loosely be described as secularisation – the process whereby religious thinking, practices and institutions lose social significance. Although it is in no sense a homogenous western phenomenon (the growth of fundamentalisms, New Age and new religious movements clearly indicates otherwise) one contemporary consequence seems to be a largely de-Christianised world where the essential exchange between artist and audience may no longer operate in the religious sphere. Instead, as Andrée Hayum (an art historian rather than a sociologist or theologian!) puts it, both find themselves in a world where 'established religion has lost its place as a dynamic and broadly based tradition, and liturgical practice has been tamed and even trivialized'.[4]

A third feature of our culture with profound consequences for the relationship between religion and the visual arts (indeed all the arts) is 'postmodernity' itself. One of its salient features – much discussed by art critics such as Donald Kuspit[5] – is a so-called crisis in representation, whereby we no longer view artistic form as a repository of perceptual customs and experiences shared by the artist and ourselves. This is not only because of the current critical tendency – which has also made its impact on theology – to view the form and content of a work of art as essentially structured by its readers and perceivers. It is also because today, as James Martin has characterised the process, 'all the frameworks of narrative description employed in the history and interpretation of both art and religion as well as all previous identifications of beauty and holiness as categories of interpretation ... are dissolved in the acids of modernity'.[6] One consequence may be that those contemporary artists most determined to demonstrate both their vehement denial of aesthetic autonomy and their determination to deconstruct the political and social myths of 'high art' are very unlikely to be practitioners of religious art, however broadly interpreted. Put differently, even if the postmodernist interpretation of our culture has already become somewhat clichéd, glib and *déjà vu*, it nonetheless exposes a culture which may already be witnessing what A.C. Danto, following Hegel, has called 'the philosophical disenfranchisement of art'[7] and in which therefore religious art has no presence and no function.

A third strand in this discussion turns on the art-historical evidence presented throughout this book, which documents – as does the history of Christianity itself – the increasingly second-order status of the visual within at least the Western Christian tradition. Even what Père Couturier called his 'very simple idea' – that 'to keep Christian art alive, every generation must appeal to the masters of living art'[8] – seems, fifty years on, hopelessly archaic. Not only is such an appeal rarely made; it is even more rarely met. It is not simply that today's 'masters' have, with some rare exceptions, emancipated themselves from religious orthodoxies and institutions. It may also be that in a historically evolved situation where many contemporary artists seem deaf or hostile to religious subject matter, where the cognitive deconstruction of art *and* religion appears to be gathering pace, where both are more often matters of private experience rather than public affirmation, and where one of the essential prerequisites for religious art may be a religious culture itself, it is indeed tempting to abandon any visual mode of religious apprehension altogether. If, too, we are caught between, on the one hand, our post-Enlightenment predisposition to separate image and reality, and, on the other, if the postmodernists are right, with an art (possible all art) purged of its referential forms, then we can surely have very little room for aesthetic or theological manoeuvre. Less theoretically, how, today, are we to restore the intimate and intricate relation between image and idea which, as earlier chapters have made clear, has traditionally characterised religious art?

However, even such a relatively dispiriting cultural context for contemporary religious art as that outlined above may not necessarily be leading to its terminal decline. For one thing, it might be as well to remind ourselves, as Burch Brown does, that 'the art that has the greatest significance is not necessarily the art of institutional religion but rather the art which happens to discern what religion in its institutional or personal focus needs most to see'.[9] What those needs might be is less clear, as is also how they might most readily be met. Clearly one way is through art's not wholly impaired capacity to disclose the transcendent. As Rudolf Otto remarked, in a famous passage in *The Idea of the Holy*, 'in great art the point is reached at which we may no longer speak of the magical but are rather confronted by the numinous itself'.[10] And even a tough-minded art historian of the younger generation like Hayum can still find herself describing the Isenheim altarpiece as 'stimulating our own surviving impulse towards the sacred sphere; we as modern viewers still sense those charismatic sources and mythic roots of its visual expression'.[11]

Hence today's artists are – unlike Grünewald – far more likely to disclose the broadly numinous rather than the explicitly incarnational, and are far more likely to offer us generalised religious experience rather than Christian revelation. In doing so they, like Rothko and other abstract expressionists before them, move religious art beyond its traditionally didactic and narrative intentions towards the primarily experiential. Some, like Mark

Tobey for example, consciously seek to purge their work of referential forms, so that through the minimal articulation of means they can pose the broadest statements and questions of meaning. Others, like Richard Long, with his emblematic orderings of natural objects *en plein air*, have gone some way towards meeting Père Couturier's plea for a more vivid apprehension of the sacred 'in terms of place and object'.

It is tempting, of course, to see such art as doing little more than providing a kind of undemanding spiritual massage for an overwhelmingly post-Christian clientele. Yet paradoxically such art also goes back to highly traditional Christian roots. For, like those who decorated Roman catacombs or carved simple Anglo-Saxon communal crosses, it also operates at differing levels of address simultaneously. Furthermore, many of today's artists, whether committed to religious subject matter or not, surely reassert through their direct appeal to visual perception (what Robert Hewison has described, apropos Ruskin, as 'the argument of the eye'[12]), as opposed to the verbal lessons of a text, the primacy of the eye over the Word in the sacramental economy. In this sense, while, as we shall see, their medium may sometimes be relatively esoteric, their message may represent a genuine democratising of religious art, not merely in terms of widening public access to the transcendent, but in affirming what Burch Brown affirms as 'the right of any religious tradition to formulate certain aesthetic theories especially appropriate to its own religious understanding'.[13]

At present Western 'religious' art seems to be giving out several confusing, if not necessarily conflicting, signals simultaneously.

One is a movement away from a narrowly and exclusively Christian art towards what the Australian critic Rosemary Crumlin has described as 'works which are only implicitly religious in their inspiration and so without identifiable religious themes or traditional symbols'.[14] A transition, in short, *away* from religion and *towards* spirituality – itself a major shift in cultural history. A second consequence is that today's artists now search for meaning within themselves rather than from supernatural stories or the rituals of institutional churches. As Diana Apostolos-Cappadona has acutely observed, 'modern artists now have the singular opportunity of *presencing* the spiritual significance of the totality of human experience in their recognition of the foundational necessity of the religious imagination'.[15] When that opportunity has been taken, the aesthetic consequences are often powerful, even disturbing, and sometimes profound. Three widely differing contemporary artists will serve as examples of this process.

The American video and installation artist Bill Viola[16] was born in 1951. The Episcopalian Christianity of his childhood was transformed by his encounter, as a student, with the poems of St John of the Cross, which, he recalls, awakened him to the possibility of 'self-perfection' as opposed to 'social perfection' and led him to seek 'liberation of the soul as well as the body', and then, subsequently, to the teachings of Zen masters and the Sufi mystics. It is unsurprising, therefore, that he writes (apropos his *The Passions*) 'true inner perception is not derived from any outer perception, as is ordinary imagination, which simply reshuffles impressions and is as limited as the senses. Rather it is seeing the inner image directly through the inner eye or *basirah*.[17] His parallel visual 'formation' is rooted heavily, and at times quite directly, in the devotional art of the late Middle Ages and the early Renaissance – Giotto, Piero della Francesca, Grünewald, Bosch and, above all, Bouts – rather than, say, Mannerism or German Expressionism. The former, for Viola, not only 'make sense in profound ways', with 'birth and death: the two fundamental images in Christian art'. They also carry a highly charged spiritual dimension. He sees that they 'were painting light as well as space' and understands that in painting light they were registering the presence of the Divinity – something he consciously strives to reflect in his own work, especially in and on water. Indeed his use of very advanced image technology serves highly traditional ends. Throughout his work (especially in 'The Messenger' (*Figure 14*) and 'The Passion') water falls, water rises; matter coalesces, substance dissolves; fire engulfs, fire consumes. For Viola, fire and water represent means of purification, just as they do in much religious iconography, but he also makes use of both elements technically as devices to dissolve and meld his moving images.

Not for the first time in the history of religious art, secular means serve sacred ends. In Viola's case there is both a public and a private agenda. Although he has always acknowledged that much of his visual language is strongly Christian, he is quick to point out (as he did recently to the film-maker Mark Kidel) that 'Christians don't own the resurrection, the crucifixion, the visitation, the deposition. These are elements of human life that have been utilised by all great traditions.'[18] Viola also believes that while most of the outward forms of religious practice have been discarded in the West, the images that move people remain the same: 'the beauty of it is', he says 'that you can use an image of a man floating out of the water or bursting into flames, and it stirs. It's hard-wired into the system.' Hence for him 'the most important place where my work exists is not in the museum gallery, or in the screening room, or on the television, and not even on the video screen itself, but in the mind of the viewer who has seen it'.[19] In this – very postmodern – sense the work does not belong to the artist, but lives instead in the consciousness of whoever views it, to bring about new thoughts and the possibility of inner transformation. For Viola himself it is possible to detect a more personal agenda – to seek a direct knowledge of God without the trappings of dogma, or a *via positiva* where the emphasis is upon what John Henry Newman called an intellectual 'Grammar of Assent', and to opt instead for 'self-knowledge' based on a *via negativa*, and recognise the permanent absence of a transcendental God.

The British sculptor Anthony Gormley,[20] born in 1950, is almost the same age as Bill Viola, and has a comparable early religious trajectory. He was born into a devout Roman Catholic family (indeed his parents gave him the initials AMDG – *Ad Maiorem Dei Gloriam*; For the Greater Glory of God!) and received a Benedictine boarding-school education. From this, he recalls, he duly 'escaped'; after reading social anthropology and art history at Cambridge, he travelled to India, where he spent nearly two years with the Buddhist meditation teacher Goenka. It was only on his return to England that he began his formal art school education, which extended over five years.

Although these brief biographical details give no more than a hint of the intellectual complexity, clarity of mind, and sheer cerebral intensity of Gormley's work, as it has evolved, they nonetheless provide some of its crucial preconditions. Although a lapsed Catholic, he clearly acknowledges his spiritual roots, and in the Phaidon monograph on his work he quotes a favourite passage from the *Confessions* of St Augustine on the subject of memory: 'A spreading limitless room within me. Who can reach its uttermost depth? Yet it is a faculty of my soul and belongs to my nature. In fact I cannot totally grasp all that I am. Thus the mind is not large enough to contain itself.'[21] Furthermore, while recognising, in a conversation with E.H. Gombrich, that 'authority has shifted from an external validation to an internal one, and I would regard that as the great joy of being an artist',[22] he also acknowledges that

> religion tries to deal with big questions, and I hope my art tries to deal with big questions like 'who are we?', 'where are we going?' The fact is that I grew up within a Christian tradition: those things are part not only of my intellectual make-up but images of self that were given to me as a child.[23]

The same Catholic trace elements are there, too, in his essentially sacramental understanding of the human body, itself the focus of so much of his work. He may have rejected Christian dogma, but he has not entirely abandoned the incarnational truth of a God who takes on human flesh.

Gormley's exposure to Buddhism is also pivotal. In India the *vipassana* form of meditation practice that Gormley studied is based on awareness and attention, eschews metaphysical speculation, and encourages the development of *sati* or 'mindfulness', a kind of unselfconscious awareness of the present moment. *Vipassana* meditation brings attention to bear on the ways in which ideas and sensations arise and disappear: thus, it is claimed, detachment and freedom are generated. Gormley has often spoken of the influence of such training on the making of his sculpture, especially in its stress on the development of 'awareness' of the body. But what really provides a 'religious' context for much of his work is more than a combination of Catholic metaphysics and Buddhist meditative practice where the body becomes all that we are. It is also an arena where the tensions between the reluctant acceptance of the body as a temporary home for the spirit and its enthusiastic celebration as one of the wonders of creation (both Catholic constructs) or as the locus of 'impermanence' and 'non-self' (both basic Buddhist constructs) are identified but never resolved.

In this sense Gormley's work is visual theology of some complexity. It also carries at least four other broadly religious motifs. One is a sense of aching after the transcendent. 'When you stand beneath a mature oak, or look at a glacial lake or at a mountain, there is, he writes,

> a sense of being held in the presence of something that is greater in terms of time and more resilient in terms of space, rooted, present, and the present-ness of that perception enters into your being. I think works of art aspire to this condition of present-ness and so can endow the viewer with this heightened sense of self.[24]

The second motif is what one critic has called Gormley's 'obsession with grand emotive issues'[25] such as birth, death and especially man alone with his fate. Indeed a recurring image in his work is a solitary person, turned, Friedrich-like, away from the viewer and facing open, natural expanses of water or sky, or marooned, in existential limbo, within the flooded crypt of Winchester Cathedral (*Figure 15*). The third is the artist's concern with the idea of presence, not in an incarnational or transcendental sense, but simply posing the basic question, 'can we have presence without the God?'[26] In this context his 'Angel of the North' is an attempt at an affirmative answer to a leading theological question. Behind it is a determination to create what he describes as 'an image that is open enough to be interpreted widely, that has multiple and generative potential for meaning but is strong enough to be a focus'. But, he asks, 'how do we construct such an image? In its being someone's can it become everyone's?' Finally, there is his urge – and the underlying rationale for the visually overwhelming 'Field for the British Isles' (with its 35,000 terracotta figures) – to demonstrate that we *are*, as a species, still able to be moved. So long as we are able to *feel*, there is hope. Gormley's own reflections on this are worth setting out verbatim. 'When we are touched', he asks,

> what part of us is moved? Is it our minds, our spirits or our souls? And what is the difference? I'm afraid I don't have much interest in the eternal soul – at least it's not much use just now – but the spirit: that part of us that is quickened when something really gets to us I have great respect for. An adventure in proving the existence of the spirit in the post-modern deconstructive age was what 'Field' turned out to be.[27]

It is an adventure in which he remains totally engaged.

Both Viola's and Gormley's work illustrates how broadly spiritual themes rather than explicitly confessional narratives have become the primary focus of contemporary religious art. This is itself one indicator of a more general mutation within Western religion itself. Its consequences for the visual arts have sometimes led (not least in North America) to artistic theorising and productions of mind-numbing vacuity and triviality, often fuelled by an overeagerness to assume that almost any artist who appears to question the meaning of life is thereby committing a religious act. There remain, however, a few artists who are prepared to ask spiritual questions first, and then give *religious* answers to them. One of these is the Scottish painter Craigie Aitchison.[28]

Born in 1926, trained at the Slade School of Art, and with an established reputation as a painter of portraits and still life, Aitchison turned to painting the Crucifixion in about 1958. Although he has something of a religious background – his grandfather was a United Free Church minister for over fifty years – Aitchison does not think that this has any bearing on why he paints Crucifixions ('but of course it could have', he has said), nor does he have any specific religious affiliation or beliefs, 'I paint crucifixions the way other people paint trees.' He has said, 'I'm recording an event, not trying to win people to Christ. But if I do, that's great.' Yet there is no doubt that Aitchison's religious feelings are genuine and profound, though not confined to Christianity. It is probable, Andrew Lambirth has suggested, that 'he uses its iconography because it has been familiar to him from earliest childhood, and thus with all its associations serves better than anything else as a focus for those feelings; and also because the imagery is traditional and universally understood, it is a suitable vehicle for communicating them.' It is also likely that his exposure, in 1954, while on an Italian government scholarship (where he also returned from Italy via Munich, Amsterdam and Brussels) to so much Gothic and Renaissance art, often in the very churches that commissioned them, made him realise that a whole world of feelings, with which he had not hitherto known how to deal, could be channelled into these subjects, above all that of the Crucifixion (*Figure 16*). This image, already loaded with associations, ideas and meanings could be recharged with his own deepest, most intense emotions, by means of shapes and colours – his natural language for everything – in a way for which no other subject provided the opportunity. It was also, as he has sometimes said, both the greatest human event he could imagine, and 'the most horrific story I have ever heard'. Hence, as Andrew Lambirth has suggested, 'Aitchison's Crucifixions can have an eschatological, apocalyptic feel to them. By no means all serene, they can be complicated with passion, or simplified with compassion. They are formidable pictorial images that work on a number of layers, as much visceral as spiritual.'[29]

Aitchison has always painted the figure of Christ from imagination, never from a model. Inevitably, his imagination is furnished with memories, and so, every conceivable pose for the subject having been invented long ago, although his way of painting it is unique, the pose must always awaken powerful iconographic echoes, both for artist and for spectator. The effect is twofold: a sense of the comforting authority of visual and religious tradition, however obscurely felt, and also, simultaneously, what Helen Lessore has called 'the timeless, non-historical quality' of his Crucifixions, which are 'both symbol and reality, in an eternal present'. Yet there is no historical or narrative element to his Crucifixions, nor need the image relate only to specifically Christian expectations and experience.

Indeed one interesting question turns on the function, popularity and effectiveness of Aitchison's multiple versions of the Christ image (120 at the last count) in a largely post-Christian culture. One reason may be that, although his Crucifixion paintings, as we have already suggested, clearly reawaken folk memories of traditional Christian iconography for many, they also neglect many of the narrative elements of the story that depictions of it historically emphasise. The traditional participants of the event are never in attendance, and Christ himself is barely present. This may be one source of their strength, in that Aitchison's presentation of Christ is unconventional and indiscernibly human. It is a bleak vision of the human form, but also one that for many is also distinctly spiritual because it so well conveys what lies behind that form. Theologically speaking, it attempts to comment upon the *ousia* of Christ.

A second explanation may lie in Aitchison's strong sense, and use, of colour. Believing that realism destroys reality, his Crucifixions hold decoration and representation in equal regard. His approach here brings to mind Max Weber's comment that 'The imagination or conception of an arrangement of forms or of a particular gamut of colour in a given rectangle is not a matter of means, but an inner spiritual vision.'[30] Hence Aitchison shows us that the spiritual is better accessed through the inspired than the observed.

A third, and final, reason for the continuing power and efficacy of his *re*-presentation of *the* most traditional Christian image of all to Western, postmodern, culture is this. His portrayal of the Christ-figure as someone 'dwarfed and isolated, lost almost in a vast God-forsaken wilderness', resonates very explicitly indeed with our current sense of the utter fragility of the human condition. In doing so within the traditional parameters of Christian art, Aitchison could also be described, not over-fancifully, as an artistic exponent of 'radical orthodoxy' in his unerring ability to refract one form of religiosity stirring in the hidden subconscious of his generation. Backwards indeed to the future.

9

theology and the visual arts

'Theology' – and especially Christian theology – and 'the arts' – and especially the visual arts – are not two discrete entities. They can be seen rather as twin media by which the world is interpreted and represented. Both are ways of perceiving and articulating memory, aspiration, community, celebration, loss, and a heightened sense of the natural order. Both can enhance our existing perceptions, and generate fresh experiences for us. It is unsurprising, therefore, that, as we have seen throughout this book, the history of Western culture has been characterised by multiple, overlapping and shifting relationships between different kinds of theological and artistic modes of perception and expression. These have varied over time and space, ranging from an intense and intimate community of purpose (as with High Gothic, for example) to barely concealed institutional hostility (as we saw at Assy). Yet in virtually no period surveyed has the relationship been merely neutral or routine. Indeed in our own time art and theology have been perpetually forced to confront – separately and together – not only the cultural thrust of late modernity and postmodernity in general, but the immense power of 'technique' as a value in itself. Both, at their best, resist the latter. For, when falsely isolated, 'technique', as Jacques Ellul,[1] among many others, has argued, is little more than a way, especially in more advanced industrial economies, of getting results without really engaging the self. Theology and art do not get results in this way. Indeed the distinctively modern pressures represented by the dominance of technique help them both to rediscover what, as Panofsky so brilliantly demonstrated in *Gothic Architecture and Scholasticism*,[2] many medieval men and women already knew they knew – that theology finds in art a complement and not a rival in its task of understanding and giving expression to all created forms. It had a central place in Ruskin's thinking too. In this sense, therefore, good art and good theology can be powerful agents in the rebirth of an expressive celebration that is not bound by, and to, mere utility.

At the same time, good theology and good art can override the false dichotomies that so often stand in the way of such fullness of expression – dichotomies between, for example, sacred and secular 'realms', spiritual and material 'values', and the intellectual and the emotional. In doing so, they may again both find that they have a common vocation: to make inroads on the weakened and impoverished modern imagination, to break open its hidden resources and equip it for adaptation to change, for celebration, and for the envisioning of alternative futures. When they are properly engaged in this vocation, theology and art may not in fact be two separate, if related, entities, but essentially part of the same cultural enterprise after all.

In our own time, of course, such a 'joint venture' is rarely embarked upon, let alone optimised. The reasons for this are very complex. They are essentially rooted in the historical realities and deep structural tensions – concerning word and image, and the relationship of both to belief and practice – which lie at the heart of Christian and perhaps all religious aesthetics. The central question remains whether in *practice*, as well as in *theory*, art is a way of seeing and knowing which is as truth-bearing and personally transformative as the language and method of theology. Clearly the core dimensions of the historical relationship between theology and the arts – art as a source of revelation, as sacrament, as symbol of ecclesiastical hegemony, as a battleground between word and image – remain historical constants to this day. To these, however, must be added at least three other art-historical developments of especial significance to contemporary theology. Two have already been identified in our first chapter – the emergence of a genuinely religious art which does *not* set out to be iconic, and the incontrovertible fact that many of those works of greatest interest today from an artistic or religious point of view are those executed by artists independently of religious institutions.

Third, it is clear that from about 1750, art, rather than supporting and articulating church-based theology, often began to separate itself from both religious institutions and Christian theology. 'Art became', as Max Weber noted, 'a cosmos of more and more consciously grasped independent values which exist in their own right ... taking over the functions of a this-worldly salvation', competing directly with religion, and 'transforming judgements of moral intent into judgements of taste.'[3] In such a context art easily becomes a manifestation, to repeat Tillich's phrase (cited earlier), of 'one form of the latent church'. Hence art has come to be treated as a source of truth, including theological truth, in its own right. Through art we see not only certain connections with culture and its traditions. We also see aspects of a judgement on that culture which is necessarily part of any significant artistic expression. The semantic system of art (like that of theology) offers order and orientation, as all signs do, provided one has learned the conventional cultural responses to them. As the historian Morse Peckham puts it, 'from the late nineteenth century ... art became itself the mythological explanation which subsumed the self. Art becomes redemptive'.[4] In our own day the complex relationship between theology and the visual arts, although grounded in the historical and cultural preconditions already outlined, is acted out principally in three critical areas – those of meaning, representation and belief.

meaning

Modernity, at least thus far, has, according to some interpretations, been relatively antagonistic to dimensions of the transcendent in human thought and experience, and its later phases (loosely labelled postmodernity) even more so. As Peter Berger[5] and others have argued, there has been a weakening of the plausibility of religious prescriptions of reality among large numbers of people in many Western societies. Indeed it is no accident that counter-modernising trends and movements have frequently been characterised by powerful reaffirmations of transcendence – what Eliade has called 'hierophanies' or manifestations of the sacred, experienced as the breaking in of another reality into the secular reality of ordinary life. The arts, and especially the visual arts, are self-evidently part of this process. Nevertheless the absence of a shared symbolic order remains a major cultural characteristic of our time. Even the ultra-acerbic art critic Peter Fuller[6] (an avowed agnostic for much of his life) looked back to when institutional religion provided just such an order. His belief was that, at certain periods, even when this order was disintegrating, artists supplied consolation for its loss in the form of work whose purpose was to transfigure the world of visual experience and thereby reconcile humanity to it.

Yet today there is often an indifference both to the meaning of such art and, even more, to its historical context. Since the twentieth century at least (if not several decades earlier), the stories and institutional practices, the imperatives and texts, which shape artists and their work (even when they suppose themselves to be searching for meaning within themselves) have increasingly differed or detached themselves from those Christian forms and content which might have shaped them. Their work tends to be individualistic and even autobiographical. There is rarely any communal, let alone liturgical, imperative nowadays for the use of biblical narrative as a point of departure.

Artists, as we have seen, feel perfectly capable of expressing religious feelings and religious perceptions without any explicit confessional commitment, and it is clear that many of today's artists are still searching for some spiritual meaning in their work above and beyond the truth of what they see.

Yet can any 'religious' work of art still be meaningful in a postmodern West when the great synthesis of meaning no longer exists? Yes, in the sense that the most appropriate role model for the contemporary artist may not necessarily be to profess a specific confessional commitment, nor to try to lift the still-pervasive taboo against explicit narrative content. It might rather be to testify – visually – to the complexities, ambiguities, disruptions and fragmentations that have characterised much modern and postmodern experience, and also, of course, much traditional and contemporary religious experience. This is, of course, a task already being undertaken by many theologians.

representation

The encouragement of thematically intentional and repre-sentational works of religious art in our own time creates a profound aesthetic dilemma. Historically, as we have already seen, Christian art in its many varieties has done more than is commonly recognised in giving form to Christian conscious-ness and direction to Christian activity – far more, perhaps, than many theological statements! But it is also the case that much overtly representational art – such *bondieuserie* – especially within the Roman Catholic tradition seems to indicate that we continue to live at a time when the normative, if archaic, forms and images of the Judaeo-Christian tradition are still (as David Morgan[7] has so ably shown) wholly accessible to the popular imagination. Indeed they can persist for centuries as media for formative memories which can also act as fertile soil for new improvisations on Christian faith, as in liberation theology and many forms of Pentecostalism. At the same time, however, the aesthetic consequences (the unadulterated kitsch) of such pervasive visual historicism, so often leads to what Paul Tillich so caustically called a 'sentimental, beautifying naturalism ... the feeble drawing, the poverty of vision, the petty historicity of our church-sponsored art'. This, he says, 'is not simply unendurable but incredible.... It calls for iconoclasm.'[8] It will not, however, receive it.

Yet the alternative, for many contemporary Western artists, involves deliberately sidestepping any literal depiction of the religious narrative. The prevailing aesthetic is now too narrow to permit it, proceeding, as it does, away from any or all literary content towards the 'universal' art of abstraction. Such abstraction, while it remains the dominant cultural mode, will continue to create and sustain a 'religious' art shorn of all symbols or imagery, and therefore without any specific doctrinal allusions whatsoever. At the same time, for very many people, much abstract art (which can now claim to be regarded as the most pervasive artform of our time – at least in the West) still remains psychologically inaccessible. This is not only because we continue to think of art as primarily representation or ornament, but also because non-representational art has yet to project, through its iconography, any universally intelligible symbolism. Hence, unsurprisingly, a substantial alternative tradition, based on the human figure, is currently being rediscovered – not least by artists such as the American George Segal, and in Britain by Anthony Gormley (as we have seen), Mark Wallinger and Peter Howson. As a result, explicit thematic content – or even narration – is no longer regarded, especially by younger artists, as pure archaism, or a regrettably retrograde element in their work. This partial lifting of the aesthetic taboo against the figurative and narrative may also carry theological significance so long as biblical narrative remains close to the central core of Christianity.

Either way, wherever religion exists, its symbols – mental, visual, dramatic – are in constant use. Therefore what symbols *do* we reinhabit or appropriate for contemporary religious contexts, and what qualities are necessary to make such symbols fruitful within our own religious experience? Are there still distinctive symbolic forms which serve in human experience to relate humanity to ultimate mystery? Certainly, in the earlier experience of the Christian Church, symbolic forms of this kind gained recognition and served to bind people to one another within a common relatedness to God through Christ. It is true that they underwent countless varieties of transformation in the succeeding centuries of Christianity. But until comparatively recently they retained a significant place – some would say *the* most significant place – in the life and culture of Western civilisation. The crucial question today – and indeed one implicit theme of this book – is whether such symbols can any longer configure and refigure reality in the modern secular and scientific world. Have they wholly lost their focus, power and meaning?

belief

One of John Ruskin's strongest convictions was that the supreme value of art lay in its disclosure, through aesthetic contemplation, of spiritual and ethical insights that one could not reach in any other kind of way. Yet much of the last hundred years has been a time when, in the West at least, cumulative empirical evidence has pointed to both the loss of religious beliefs and the apparent paradox of normative agnosticism combined with continuing religious needs. In such circumstances it is difficult to refashion religious art – whether representational or non-representational – when people often do not have an organic, meaningful relationship with it. There is no overarching symbolic world to inhabit. More specifically, as the cultural critic John Berger[9] has argued, the cultural changes accompanying the arrival of modernity are not just a question of improved technologies, such as faster transport, quicker messages, a more complex scientific vocabulary, higher accumulation of capital under markets, and where human identity is predicated as much – *pace* Marx – by our relationship to consumption as to production. They also appear to establish new circumstances, described by George Steiner[10] as 'where God's presence is no longer a tenable supposition and where His presence is no longer a felt, indeed overwhelming weight, [and] certain dimensions of thought and creativity are no longer attainable.' How, therefore, he asks, can we encounter that real presence which great art ('touched', in his phrase, 'by the fire and ice of God') has to offer? In general, he suggests, 'we must look on the world *as if* created and respond to it *as if* to the "real presence of the transcendental" and, especially in an era of secularisation, the artist must "make a wager on transcendence".' In this sense, movements such as Cubism or Abstract Expressionism might be interpreted more as a creative response to the loss of transcendence than as a celebration of it, more of an attempt to reopen rather than to close the space in which God and 'the spirit' can be recognised. But the vexed question of how to do so, without confusing the aesthetic with the religious, and without making an idol out of art, remains problematic, if not impossible.

theological responses

As indicated at the outset of this chapter, the arts – and especially the visual arts – if not always historically interdependent with theology, are clearly a parallel activity to it and are sometimes indistinguishable from it. Indeed in our own time, when both Christian theology and the visual arts often pose and present themselves as a series of questions rather than a pattern of answers, both the fundamental character of Christian belief and the so-called Western tradition in art are being examined and challenged. One could go further and suggest that theology in isolation from the arts is starved of concrete embodiments of its insights into the fullness of human life. Art can give theology the eyes to see ourselves in all our dimensions, and the ears to hear the voice of our inner lives, and one of the instruments with which to communicate with each other. From such a perspective, the languages of theology, too, are themselves a matter of determining the structures by which people have defined their relation to the world and responded to their apprehension of the manifestations of the divine. In this sense, to do theology is not to know God in a particularly modern way, but to respond to God through the weight and structure and purpose of a given language. That language should, where possible, be both verbal and visual, embodying both a theology of the arts and art as an expression of theology. In practical terms it suggests no less than making art an integral component of theological education, and theology an integral component of art education. In such a context it might be useful to identify the responses of some representative twentieth-century theologians to the arts by locating them along the threefold continuum developed by John Dillenberger in his ground-breaking *A Theology of Artistic Sensibilities* (1986).[11]

At one end is the position where 'no relation is seen between the arts and theological work'. Here, except among one or two wholly unreconstructed biblical literalists, determinedly opposed to any form of 'graven image', it is difficult to identify many who deny *any* such relationship – although there are many who, for a variety of reasons, pay almost no attention to any of the arts. Karl Barth is, of course, an interesting test case. He was intensely musical, writing a monograph on Mozart – who, he says, 'although not especially good or especially pious, *heard* the peace that passes all understanding'. Barth likened the kingdom of God to a composition by Mozart which is at once 'beautiful play' and 'virtually the equivalent of a parable'.[12] But Barth's attitude to the visual arts was different, especially in the context of worship. He maintained that 'images and symbols have no place *at all* in a building designed for Protestant worship.'[13] Yet art could, like John the Baptist in Grünewald's Isenheim altarpiece (a picture that much preoccupied Barth), witness by pointing in the direction of the revelation of God in the person of Jesus Christ. Barth was, however, deeply suspicious of any conception of art which suggested that it might somehow act as a human point of contact for experience of God. He was well aware of the temptation to find in the aesthetic sphere an unduly privileged mediation of the divine (especially when, as in modern Western culture, the intellectual and practical significance of God is so often dismissed). In any case, Barth's relationship to natural theology, to liberal Protestantism, and especially to Schleiermacher, was itself complex and ambiguous, and part of his response was to perceive the arts as often being appropriated, almost idolatrously, by them. In sum it could be said that Barth found no necessary, intrinsic or systematic relationship between art and theology, although, for Barth, God remains, of course, free to witness to himself through the arts.

At a mid-point along Dillenberger's continuum is where 'a positive relation is articulated, sometimes successfully and sometimes not'. One powerful source of this approach can be found in Rudolf Otto's seminal *The Idea of the Holy*, already drawn upon in Chapter 5. Especially significant for the present discussion is his comparison between religious experiences of the numinous and aesthetic experience of the beautiful – a relationship which for him was more than mere analogy. He believed, too, in the power of the abstract to convey numinous experience, suggesting that there are, especially in oriental art, very many pictures, especially those connected with contemplation, which impress the observer with the feeling that the void itself is depicted as a subject, is indeed the main subject of the picture. Otto argued that this pictorial emptiness was similar to the void spoken of by the mystics. 'For void', he wrote, 'is, like darkness and silence and rejection, but a negation that does away with every "this" and "here" in order that the "wholly other" may become actual.'[14]

Pre-eminent, and perhaps most influential here, is Paul Tillich, for whom the visual, like all aspects of human life, belongs to the world with which theology is concerned. In a highly suggestive essay entitled 'On the Theology of Fine Art and Architecture' Tillich observes that it is natural for a theologian to raise the two questions, 'How is the aesthetic function of the human spirit related to the religious function? How are artistic symbols – and all artistic creations are symbols, however naturalistic their styles may be – related to the symbols in which religion expresses itself?'[15] Tillich's answer is that there is no style which excludes the artistic expression of 'ultimate concern', as the ultimate is not bound to any special form of things or experiences. Indeed 'the ultimate is present in experiences in which not only reality is experienced, but in the encounter itself with reality'.[16] In practice Tillich does not develop a systematic analysis of the relationship between religion and art. Rather, he presents a series of separate studies intended to disclose the way in which particular artefacts can be interpreted as expressions of ultimate concern. 'Art', he maintains, 'indicates what the character of a spiritual situation is: it does this more immediately and directly than do science or philosophy, for it is less burdened by objective considerations.'[17]

Although Tillich's analysis of the relationship between artistic styles and religion in general – in terms of subject matter, form and style – is clear and relatively persuasive, and his central contention that when 'once more religion is without a home within man's spiritual life, it looks around for another spiritual function to join ... namely the aesthetic'[18] is initially plausible, several difficulties remain. One is that Tillich's discussion of art, especially in his *Systematic Theology*, is limited by the relative restriction of his remarks to the role that art plays in the life of the institutional church. More critically, his contention that 'the rediscovery of the expressive element in art since about 1900 is a *decisive event* for the relation of religion and the visual arts. It has made religious art possible again'[19] surely overplays the role of Expressionism, even Abstract Expressionism, at the expense of purely abstract art and other twentieth-century movements? Ironically, as both Dillenbergers have pointed out, Tillich's heavy reliance on 'expressionism' in art actually hindered him from 'seeing precisely those facets in contemporary art which accorded with his own viewpoint'.[20] The work of abstract expressionists like Mark Rothko, Adolf Gottlieb and Barnett

Newman resonates with expressions of the tragic, the sublime, the demonic – all elements familiar to Tillich's own cultural analysis.[21] Nonetheless, of all twentieth-century theologians, he certainly set the agenda for the role of the arts in theological inquiry most explicitly.

Tillich's approach to art is echoed and developed in at least one antithetical quarter – in the work of Karl Rahner. In an important and somewhat neglected essay,[22] he raises the question of whether or not the visual arts can be left out of theological activity. What shall we do, he asks, about the non-verbal arts – architecture, sculpture, painting and music? If they are 'human self-expressions which embody one way or another the process of human self-discovery', do they not 'have the same value and significance as the verbal arts?' If that is the case, and

> if as insofar as theology is man's reflexive self-expression about himself in the light of divine revelation we could propose the thesis that theology cannot be complete until it appropriates these arts as an integral moment of itself and its own life, until the arts become an intrinsic moment of theology itself.... They communicate something about what the human being really is in the eyes of God which cannot be completely translated into verbal theology.... If theology is simply and arbitrarily defined as being identical with verbal theology, then of course we cannot say that. But then we would have to ask whether such a reduction of theology to verbal theology does justice to the value and uniqueness of these arts, and whether it does not unjustifiably limit the capacity of the arts to be used by God in this revelation.

It is precisely in contending that the non-verbal provides what cannot be totally translated into verbal theology that Rahner ensures art's necessary place. For him art and theology, different and related, are both rooted in humanity's transcendent nature.

Other contemporary theologians have extended the argument further. Ray Hart argues that the arts should be taken as seriously as metaphysics. For him 'they are not an adjunct to the verbal but provide, as do other modalities, fundamental clues as to what we are and what we are becoming'.[23] John Cobb, too, responding as a theologian to André Malraux's *Metamorphoses of the Gods* (1954), sees in contemporary, especially abstract, art 'a secular development that can be positively rather than negatively understood' and argues that although explicitly Christian subject matter may have disappeared, 'the logos is now hiddenly and immanently present waiting to be named as Christ in a new form'.[24] Hans Kung, although primarily focused on art as the expression of estrangement, also claims that art functions eschatologically, so that the tree painted beautifully on canvas 'is not sealed in its reality, but rouses the hope ... that the world as it ought to be will at some time actually arise'[25] – a hope, in short, for a new heaven and a new earth.

Finally, Mark C. Taylor, for all his theological attempts at deconstructive atheism, successfully shows how in the history of art the death of God, followed by the loss of the self and the transition from transcendence to immanence, may be culturally documented. In his *Disfiguring* (1992) he clearly shows precisely how religious presuppositions have informed modern artistic theory and also how the visual arts continue to act as a rich source for the theological imagination. If his conclusion is somewhat bleak, in that the purest expressions of postmodern art, and architecture too, are, for him, no more than 'epiphanies of God, a God who is and only is a totally catastrophic abyss',[26] his identification of the spiritual subtext and credal coda of much twentieth-century art is both convincing and more traditionally Tillichian than he would probably admit.

The third and final point on Dillenberger's continuum of theological responses to the arts, and one already implied by Taylor, is *where the arts themselves provide paradigms and images that affect the nature of theological methods.* The question is a complex one, involving both the way art functions theologically and in what mode art is relevant to theology. It is clear, of course, that the semantic systems of both the arts and theology offer order and orientation, as all signs do, provided one has learned to participate in them. Thus a painting or piece of sculpture is, in this sense, a visual exemplification of an elaborate and wide-ranging system of explanation which regresses from the sign through a hierarchical series of explanatory regression to the single terminal explanatory term 'God'. Theology is a verbal exemplification of the same system of aesthetic apprehension. Hence we find the philosopher Nicholas Wolterstorff arguing that aesthetic delight is shared – 'a component within and a species of that joy which belongs to the shalom that God has ordained as the goal of personal and communal existence'. Therefore, he claims, 'it becomes a matter of responsible action to help make available, to ourselves and others, the experience of aesthetic delight'.[27] It is, in short, a theological as well as a moral imperative.

A more complex approach is to be found in the work of Hans Urs von Balthasar, who develops a highly sophisticated theological aesthetics, which traces analogies between Christian faith and the visual arts. This is aesthetics read theologically, and goes far beyond merely pointing out Christian themes in works of art or showing parallels between theology and painting. It is an attempt to situate our perception of objects – of that which is 'beautiful' in created being – in its unfinalisable but real relation to our perception of God's glory, which opens itself to us both in and beyond created being. Von Balthasar tries to show how, throughout history, aesthetic categories have offered illumination to Christian theologians as they have attempted to describe the cosmos, Christian life, the Kingdom and the nature and action of God.

Von Balthasar shows that aesthetics draws on what is first a contemplative stance, which is prepared to accord a primacy to the object. Aesthetics is prepared to respect the integrity of the form that is perceived, rather than trying to pull it apart so as to satisfy some alien set of questions or expectations. In other words, it is prepared to let the form of the object discipline and condition its responses. And because divine revelation, too, takes concrete form, von Balthasar sets out to emphasise the analogies between it and an aesthetic object, and the importance of a contemplative stance in each case. Then, in attending to the form, the contemplative person discovers that he or she receives the revelation (or the work of art) not as a mirror reflects an image or a blank surface receives an imprint, but by a kind of imaginative participation. The object of contemplation generates life beyond itself, and the response of the contemporary person can be a medium through which that which is contemplated is transposed into new contexts. As Burch Brown has pointed out, von Balthasar's own writing is itself an example of such transposition: a demonstration 'that theology can order its own language and reflection in such a way as to exhibit aesthetic integrity, proportion and a certain claritas befitting its objects and actions'.[28] In this sense, for von Balthasar, theology takes up the work of aesthetics at a higher level, and reveals to aesthetics its true vocation. Aesthetic contemplation reveals only fragments of form in the world. It reveals the fact that worldly forms are incomplete, partial, not self-grounding. But the object which commands theological contemplation – the revelation of God's most universal and simultaneously most concrete form – gives a centre and integrity to the many fragments, and makes the beautiful – rightly perceived – a potential medium of the 'glorious'.

At times, von Balthasar's sustained exploration of the analogies between faith and revelation on the one hand and aesthetic insights on the other can seem a little forced and overschematic. For the non-theologian, especially one who is an artist, he is rarely easy reading. Nevertheless, his is a potentially creative theological response to the arts, and one which is ever alert to the broad tasks of contemporary theology. He rightly sees, along with so many of the latter's practitioners, the importance of proceeding beyond the notion that art is theologically interesting only when it has an explicitly ecclesial function or an overtly didactic purpose.

conclusion

In a culture in which so many artists and their audiences are not interested in explicitly religious themes and there is no comprehensive religious tradition that the majority of people now inhabit and sustain, the way in which art and theology interact must remain problematic. This is, arguably, the way things are in many parts of the developed world, and although, as we have seen, Christian theologians and philosophers of religion are taking aesthetics seriously again, the essential exchange between theology and the arts (like the essential exchange between artist and audience) may not be set to take place within an identifiably 'religious' frame of reference. One reason may be that in the West at least we have seen the gradual triumph of the verbal over the visual, of word over image in the process of religious apprehension. In this sense Protestantism not only reified language as a means of communication between humanity and God. Its literal awareness of the Word also encouraged a negative theological aesthetic. 'There is every reason', says Frank Burch Brown, 'to take seriously a claim that ... the Protestant Reformers, in supplanting the Catholic emphasis on the visual with an emphasis on the aural (verbal and musical) altered a whole religious sensibility at a perceptual level.'[29]

Today, even that sensibility itself shows signs of being altered once again through the sheer superfluity of available sense data. Indeed a strong case could be made for the dominant imagery of contemporary Western culture being neither primarily visual nor verbal but essentially audiovisual – the singer Madonna rather than the Madonna – and, as Kieran Flanagan has argued, 'now increasingly "virtual"'.[30] One result is the contemporary paradox of a highly visual culture in which Christian imagery has itself become increasingly invisible.

If, then, as seems to be the case, we are caught between, on the one hand, a post-Enlightenment disposition to separate image and reality, and on the other, if the postmodern theorists are right, an art (indeed all art) purged of its referential forms, then we are faced with the very difficult challenge of restoring the intimate and intricate relation between theology and art that has traditionally characterised theological aesthetics. One way might be by the use (the re-inhabiting) of the symbols of Christian self-understanding and self-expression by means of an attentiveness to their history and a disciplined corporate practice (a kind of dress rehearsal) that reinstates them and enables them to be performed once again in new contexts. This does not mean a return to a crudely didactic or narrative use of art. But it certainly does mean a rejection of the idea that there is such a thing as 'generalised religious experience' which is always going to be most at home in the abstract. It means a recognition that faith lives from the particular, and that it was with great psychological insight that the Iconophiles in the eighth and ninth centuries defended the depiction of the Incarnate One in art, against a false notion of transcendence. The historic, the concrete and the explicitly incarnational are not the straightforward opposites of the mysterious and the numinous. Rather, as theologians like von Balthasar have done much to show us, finite forms encounter us in infinitely various ways, and can open up unfathomable reaches of meaning. The face of a human being is the medium both of what is familiar and also of what is unknown and still to be discovered: the concrete mediating the transcendent. It is no accident that one of the most traditional and enduring Christian symbols of all (as shown in the account of public responses to the 'Seeing Salvation' exhibition) is the face of Jesus Christ himself.

In more general terms, theological and artistic developments continue to remain historically and culturally interdependent, even if not necessarily integrated with the kind of incarnational theology especially prominent in affirming the validity of aesthetics   and vice versa. In this sense art can continue to enhance our theological, and indeed our religious, understanding. It reminds us that, although the traditional boundaries between the sacred and the profane may have become increasingly blurred, and although what the late Michael Camille called 'our collective repositories of immanence'[31] may be in danger of disappearing altogether, the revelation of God, and our capacity to respond to it through the medium of art, as in every dimension of life, is not yet about to vanish for ever.

notes

introduction

1. John Ruskin, *Modern Painters*, Vol. III (London 1898), p. 61.
2. Georg Simmel, *Essays on Religion* (New Haven CT, 1997), p. 77.
3. David Martin, 'Music and Religion: Ambivalence towards the Aesthetic', in *Christian Language in Its Mutations* (Aldershot, 2002), pp. 47–67.
4. Robert Wuthnow, *All in Sync* (Berkeley CA, 2003).
5. Anthony Forge (ed.), *Primitive Art and Society* (Oxford 1973); and Robert Layton, *The Anthropology of Art*, 2nd edn (Cambridge, 1991).
6. Michel and Gaby Vovelle, *Vision de la mort et de l'an delà en Provence* (Paris, 1970).
7. Colleen McDannell, *Material Christianity* (New Haven CT, 1995).
8. David Morgan, *Visual Piety* (Berkeley, 1998), and *The Sacred Gaze* (Berkeley CA, 2005).
9. Émile Mâle, *The Gothic Image* (New York, 1958).
10. Andrée Hayum, *God's Medicine and the Painter's Vision* (Princeton NJ, 1989).
11. Joseph Leo Koerner, *The Reformation of the Image* (Chicago, 2004).
12. Richard Wollheim, *Art and Its Objects*, 2nd edn (Cambridge, 1980), p. 122.

one

1. Saint John of Damascus, in *On the Divine Images*, trans. and ed. David Anderson (New York, 1980), p. 84.

2. John Kennedy Campbell, *Honour, Family and Patronage* (Oxford, 1964).

3. Margaret Kenna, 'An Anthropological Approach to Icons', paper presented to Lancaster Religious Studies Colloquium, 1977.

4. Campbell, *Honour, Family and Patronage*, p. 344.

5. Gerhard Ladner, 'Origins and Significance of the Byzantine Iconoclastic Controversy', *Medieval Studies* 2 (1940), p. 129; see also Charles Barber, *Figure and Likeness: On the Limits of Representation in Byzantine Iconoclasm* (Princeton NJ, 2002).

6. Hans Belting, *Likeness and Presence* (Chicago, 1994), p. 458.

7. Lee Palmer Wandel, *Voracious Idols and Violent Hands* (Cambridge, 1995), p. 61 and *passim*.

8. Eamon Duffy, *The Stripping of the Altars*, 2nd edn (New Haven CT, 2005), p. 480.

9. Mark Roskill (ed.), *The Letters of Van Gogh* (London, 1972), p. 151.

10. Rowan Williams, 'Christian Art and Cultural Pluralism: Reflections on *L'Art de l'icone* by Paul Evdokimov', *Eastern Churches Review*, vol. 8, no. 1 (1976), p. 42.

11. Saint Bonaventure, *The Soul's Journey into God*, trans. and ed. E. Cousins (New York, 1978), pp. 72–3.

12. Abbot Suger, *On the Abbey Church of St-Denis and its Art Treasures*, ed. E. Panofsky, 2nd edn (Princeton NJ, 1979), p. 65.

13. Friedrick Heer, *The Medieval World: Europe, 1100–1350* (London, 1962), p. 332.

14. Saint Basil, *Exegetic Homilies, On the Hexameron*, trans. A.C. Way (Washington DC, 1963), pp. 12–13.

15. Giulio Argan, *The Baroque Age* (New York, 1989), p. 81.

16. Howard Hibbard, '*Ut picturae sermones*: The First Painted Decoration of the Gesu', in R. Wittkower and I. Jaffe (eds), *Baroque Art: The Jesuit Contribution* (New York, 1972), p. 41.

17. Ibid., p. 60.

18. Ibid., p. 34.

19. Argan, *The Baroque Age*, p. 64.

20. Émile Mâle, *Religious Art* (New York, 1958), p. 198.

21. John Rupert Martin, *Baroque* (New York, 1977), p. 13.

22. Hibbard, '*Ut picturae sermones*', p. 55.

23. Ibid., p. 39.

24. John Tinsley, 'Art and the Church: A Theologian's Viewpoint', in P. Burman and K. Nugent (eds), *Prophecy and Vision* (Bristol, 1982).

25. The term 'tradition-directed' is drawn from the three categories devised by the sociologist David Riesman in *The Lonely Crowd* (Boston MA, 1952) to typify the historical relationship of culture to conduct in American society. The other two categories are 'inner' and 'other' directed.

26. Edgar Wind, *Pagan Mysteries of the Renaissance* (London, 1967).

27. William Rubin, *Modern Sacred Art and the Church of Assy* (New York, 1961). See also John Dillenberger, 'Artists and Commissions: The Church at Assy revisited', in Diana Apostolos-Cappadona, *Art, Creativity and the Sacred*, rev. edn (New York, 1995), pp. 193–204.

28. Paul Tillich, *Theology of Culture* (Oxford, 1959), p. 74.

29. David Morgan (ed.), *Icons of American Protestantism: The Art of Warner Sallman* (New Haven CT, 1996).

30. For 'Our Lady of Guadelupe', see David Brading, *Mexican Phoenix* (Cambridge, 2001). For the 'Lord of the Miracles', see Jeffrey Klaiber, *The Catholic Church in Peru, 1821–1985: A Social History* (Washington DC, 1992).

31. Richard Temple, *Icons: Divine Beauty* (London, 2004), p. 208.

32. Harold Rosenberg, *Tradition and the New* (New York, 1960), p. 210.

33. Hans Kung, *Art and the Question of Meaning* (London, 1981), pp. 30–31.

34. Paul Gauguin, *Letters to His Wife and Friends* (London, 1966), p. 224.

35. Max Weber, *The Rational and Social Foundations of Music* (Urbana, 1957), p. 117.

two

1. *Report of the Select Committee on Art Unions* (London, 1845), pp. 331–5.

2. Trevor Fawcett, *The Rise of English Provincial Art* (Oxford, 1974), p. 212.

3. The debate, and its visual consequences, are fully described in Thomas Boase, 'The Decoration of the New Palace of Westminster', *Journal of the Warburg and Courtauld Institutes* 17 (1954), pp. 319–67.

4. William Powell Frith, *My Autobiography and Reminiscences* (London, 1890), pp. 251–2.

5. Benjamin Robert Haydon, *Diary, 1825–32*, ed. W.B. Pope (Boston MA, 1963), p. 547.

6. Samuel Redgrave, *Catalogue to the Sheepshanks Collection* (London, n.d.), p. 19.

7. John Ruskin, *Academy Notes*, ed. Laurence Binyon (London, 1906), p. 187. An excellent critical account of Ruskin's religious opinions can be found in Michael Wheeler, *Ruskin's God* (Cambridge, 1999), esp. chs 3 and 5.

8. Dante Gabriel Rossetti, *Letters and Memoir*, 2 vols (London, 1895), Vol. I, p. 153.

9. Algernon Graves, *Royal Academy Exhibitors, 1769–1904*, 8 vols (Bath, 1970).

10. Alasdair MacIntyre, *Secularization and Moral Change* (Oxford, 1967), *passim*.

11. Frith, *My Autobiography*, pp. 466–7.

12. Steven Marcus, *The Other Victorians* (London, 1966).

13. Basil Bernstein, *Class, Codes and Control*, 3 vols (London 1971–74).

14. See Gleeson White, *English Illustration: The Sixties* (Bath, 1970), and also Helene Roberts, 'British Art Periodicals of the 18th and 19th Centuries', in *R.S.V.P. Newsletter* 9 (1970).

15. Jeremy Maas, *Gambart: Prince of the Victorian Art World* (London, 1975), pp. 174 and *passim*.

16. Edward Armitage, *Lectures on Painting* (London, 1866), p. 71.

17. William Fredeman (ed.), *The P.R.B. Journal* (Oxford, 1975), p. 67. See also David Jasper and T.R. Wright (eds), *The Critical Spirit and the Will to Believe* (London, 1989), for some acute cross-disciplinary appraisals of this major Victorian debate.

18. John Ruskin, *Pre-Raphaelitism* (London, 1906), p. 20.

19. Fredeman (ed.), *The P.R.B. Journal*, p. 44.

20. The sculptor Henry Weekes, in his *Lectures on Art* (London, 1983), p. 121, refers to 'the weed of mannerism dominating the art of the

previous decade'.

21. Hans Gerth and C. Wright Mills (eds), *From Max Weber: Essays in Sociology* (London, 1948), p. 342.

three

1. Margaret Visser, *The Geometry of Love: Space, Time, Mystery and Meaning in an Ordinary Church* (London, 2001) is a pioneering, if somewhat overdiscursive, exception.
2. Hayum, *God's Medicine*, p. 118.
3. Gabriele Finaldi (ed.), *The Image of Christ* (London, 2000).
4. René Rémond, *Religion and Society in Modern Europe* (Oxford, 1999), p. 99.
5. William James, *The Varieties of Religious Experience* (London, 1985), p. 73.
6. Robert Wuthnow, *Creative Spirituality: The Way of the Artist* (Berkeley CA, 2001).
7. Later published in book form as Neil MacGregor, with Erika Langmuir, *Seeing Salvation: Images of Christ in Art* (London, 2000).
8. Grace Davie, 'Seeing Salvation: The Use of Text as Data in the Sociology of Religion', in Paul Avis (ed.), *Public Faith? The State of Belief and Practice in Britain* (London, 2003), pp. 28–44, documents this issue fully and perceptively, drawing upon much of the same material as the author.

four

1. Mona C. Harrison, *The Centenary History of St Matthew's Church and Parish, Northampton* (Edinburgh, 1993).
2. Walter Hussey, *Patron of Art* (London, 1985) is an indispensable, if not always reliable, source for this chapter. See reviews by Christopher Reid, *Times Literary Supplement*, 7 June 1985; and Tom Devonshire Jones, *Church Building*, May 1996. See also Michael Nicholas, *Muse at St Matthew's* (Northampton, 1968); and Garth Turner, 'Aesthete, Impresario, and Indomitable Persuader: Walter Hussey at St Matthew's, Northampton and Chichester Cathedral', in Diana Wood

(ed.), *The Church and the Arts* (Oxford, 1992), pp. 523–35.

3. Harrison, *The Centenary History*, p. 92.

4. Hussey, *Patron*, p. 23.

5. Ibid., p. 24.

6. Ibid., p. 32.

7. Ibid., p. 25.

8. Ibid., p. 26.

9. Ibid., p. 30.

10. Ibid., pp. 30–31.

11. Ibid., pp. 32–3.

12. Ibid., pp. 44–6.

13. Ibid., p. 26. It took some non-parishioners a little longer. In 1949, Sir Alfred Munnings, in his presidential speech at the Royal Academy dinner, could still refer to 'a Madonna and Child in a church in Northampton. My horses may be all wrong – we may be all wrong – but I'm damned sure *that* isn't right'. Quoted in Michael Day, *Modern Art in English Churches* (Oxford, 1984), p. 25.

14. Ibid., pp. 49–50.

15. Ibid., pp. 50–53. See also Martin Hammer, *Bacon and Sutherland* (New Haven CT, 2003), and especially his *Graham Sutherland – Landscapes, War Scenes and Portraits* (London, 2005), which reprints (pp. 376–8) Sutherland's own broadcast account of his commission for St Matthew's, originally printed in *The Listener*, 6 September 1951.

16. Hans Feibusch, *Mural Painting* (London, 1946), cited in Hussey, *Patron*, pp. 54–5.

17. Hussey, *Patron*, p. 58.

18. Ibid., p. 63.

19. Ibid., p. 65.

20. *Chichester 900* (Chichester, 1975), p. 69.

21. Quoted in Turner, 'Aesthete, Impresario', in Wood (ed.), *The Church and the Arts*, p. 533.

five

1. William Butler Yeats, 'Sailing to Byzantium', in *Collected Poems* (London, 1955), p. 218.

2. Quoted in Henry Stapleton, 'Stones that Speak', *Theology*, vol. 98, no. 792 (1996) p. 441.

3. Ian Reader and Tony Walter (eds), *Pilgrimage in Popular Culture* (London, 1993), p. 241.

4. Victor and Edith Turner, *Image and Pilgrimage in Christian Culture* (New York, 1978), pp. 249–50.

5. John Renard, 'A Method for Comparative Studies in Religious Visual Arts: Approaching Architecture', *Religion and the Arts*, vol. 1, no. 1 (1996), pp. 100–123.

6. Rudolf Otto, *The Idea of the Holy* (London, 1923), pp. 65–7.

7. Quoted in Helen and Lawrence Fowler (eds), *Cambridge Commemorated* (Cambridge, 1984), p. 254.

8. For the former see Sheila Bonde, *Fortress-Churches of Languedoc: Architecture, Religion and Conflict* (Cambridge, 1994). For the latter, see especially Henry Russell Hitchcock, *The Architecture of Henry Hobson Richardson and His Times* (Cambridge MA, 1966).

9. Christopher Lewis, 'Cathedrals: Restricting and Liberating Space', *Theology* 98 (1988), pp. 179–86; and 'Human Ebb and Flow: Cathedrals and People', in Stephen Platten and Christopher Lewis (eds), *Flagships of the Spirit* (London, 1998), pp. 140–54.

10. Martyn Percy, 'The Morphology of Pilgrimage in the Toronto Blessing', *Religion*, vol. 28, no. 3 (1998), p. 286.

11. Nicholas Lash, *The Beginning and End of Religion* (Cambridge, 1996), p. 185.

12. Quoted by Thomas Pavel, *Times Literary Supplement*, 15 March 1996, pp. 31–2.

13. Simon Coleman and Peter Collins, 'Constructing the Sacred: The Anthropology of Architecture in the World Religions', *Architectural Design*, vol. 66, no. 11/12 (1996), pp. 14–18.

14. *English Tourist Board, Annual Report 2004* (London, 2004).

15. Kieran Flanagan, *Seen and Unseen: Visual Culture, Sociology and Theology* (London, 2004), p. 157. This very suggestive study is critically appraised by Graham Howes in *New Blackfriars*, vol. 86, no. 1003 (May 2005), pp. 351–3.

16. Flanagan, *Seen and Unseen*, p. 22.

17. Martyn Percy, *Catching the Fire* (Oxford, 1997), p. 28.

18. Robert Hewison, *The Heritage Industry* (London, 1987), p. 10.

19. William Morris, quoted by Simon Jenkins, *Sunday Times*, 29 March 1994, pp. 9–10.

20. Jyoti Sahi, *Holy Ground* (Auckland, 1998), p. 16.

21. Quoted by Alison Lurie, *New York Review of Books*, 3 July 2003, p. 31.

22. André Malraux, *The Voices of Silence* (London, 1954), p. 600.

23. David Lowenthal, *The Heritage Crusade and the Spoils of History* (Cambridge, 1998), pp. 61–2.

24. Simon Jenkins, *England's Thousand Best Churches* (London, 1999), p. vii.

25. Ibid., p. xxix.

26. Françoise Gilot, *Matisse and Picasso: A Friendship in Art* (New York, 1990), p. 240.

27. Germaine Bazin, *The Museum Age* (New York, 1967), p. 7.

six

1. Barbara Raw, *Anglo-Saxon Crucifixion Iconography and the Art of the Monastic Revival* (Cambridge, 1990).

2. Jaroslav Pelikan, *Imago Dei: The Byzantine Aplogia for Icons* (New Haven CT, 1990), p. 45. See also Linda Safran (ed.), *Heaven on Earth: Art and Church in Byzantium* (Philadelphia, 2005).

3. John of Damascus, 'Orations on the Holy Icons', I. 17, in *Patrologia Graeca* (Paris, 1844–64), vol. 94, p. 1248.

4. Hayum, *God's Medicine*, pp. 61–71.

5. William Hood, *Fra Angelico at San Marco* (New Haven CT, 1993), p. 10. Hood's account is detailed, perceptive and authoritative. The bibliography is comprehensive and the end notes very informative. Lawrence Kanter and Pia Palladino, *Fra Angelico* (New Haven CT, 2005), the catalogue of the 2005 exhibition at the Metropolitan Museum of Art, New York, contains some useful contributory essays, especially that on San Marco by Magnolia Scudieri, pp. 177–9.

6. William Hood, 'Fra Angelico at San Marco: Art and the Liturgy of Cloistered Life', in Timothy Verdon and John Henderson (eds), *Christianity and the Renaissance* (Syracuse NY, 1990), p. 188.

7. Letter to Monsignor Remond, Archbishop of Nice, 21 June 1951,

which the artist requested be read out at the beginning of the ceremony. Printed in full in Marcel Billot (ed.), *The Vence Chapel: The Archive of a Creation* (Milan, 1999), Appendix 5, p. 439. Billot is an indispensable source for this section of Chapter 5. A full account of the Vence project is to be found in Hilary Spurling, *Matisse: The Master* (London, 2005) pp. 448–60.

8. Quoted by Hilary Spurling in *Matisse, His Art and His Textiles: The Fabric of Dreams* (London, 2004), p. 32.

9. Gilot, *Matisse and Picasso*, pp. 194–6.

10. See Marcel Billot (ed.), *The Vence Chapel*, where their exchanges are fully documented. For Couturier himself, see Thomas F. O'Meara, *Modern Art and the Sacred: The Prophetic Ministry of Alain Couturier*, www.spiritualitytoday.org/spir2day/863814omeara.html.

11. Rubin, *Modern Sacred Art*, p. 157.

12. Jack Flam (ed.), *Matisse on Art*, rev. edn (Berkeley, 1995).

13. See Billot (ed.), *The Vence Chapel*, pp. 47–77, for these exchanges in full.

14. Quoted in Rubin, *Modern Sacred Art*, p. 158.

15. Henri Matisse, *Chapelle du Rosaire des Dominicaines de Vence* (Vence, 1951), p. 3.

16. Marie-Alain Couturier, *Sacred Art* (Austin TX, 1989), p. 92.

17. Ibid., p. 158.

18. Billot (ed.), *The Vence Chapel*, p. 101.

19. Jane Dillenberger, *Style and Content in Christian Art* (New York, 1965), pp. 222–3.

20. Rubin, *Modern Sacred Art*, p. 157.

21. Couturier, *Sacred Art*, p. 94.

22. Quoted by Dominique Szymusiak in *Matisse, His Art and His Textiles*, p. 69.

23. Billot (ed.), *The Vence Chapel*, p. 134.

24. Gilot, *Matisse and Picasso*, p. 196.

25. James E. Breslin, *Mark Rothko* (Chicago, 1993), provides a full-scale biography of the painter. Susan J. Barnes, *The Rothko Chapel: An Act of Faith* (Austin TX, 1989), is a useful monograph with a good select bibliography. Sheldon Nodelman, *The Rothko Chapel Paintings* (Austin TX, 1992) is a more detailed description and analysis.

26. A facsimile of this letter is reproduced in Barnes, *The Rothko Chapel*, p. 18.

27. Ahearn's account is in Breslin, *Mark Rothko*, p. 651 n4.

28. Dominique de Menil, 'The Rothko Chapel', *Art Journal*, vol. 30, no. 3 (1971), pp. 249–51.

29. Quoted in Dore Ashton, *About Rothko* (New York, 1983), p. 164.

30. Quoted in Breslin, *Mark Rothko*, p. 460.

31. Ashton, *About Rothko*, p. 179.

32. Barnes, *The Rothko Chapel*, p. 44.

33. Ibid., p. 22.

34. De Menil, 'The Rothko Chapel', p. 251.

35. Mark Rothko, *The Artist's Reality*, ed. Christopher Rothko (New Haven CT, 2004).

36. Brian O'Doherty, *Art International*, vol. 14, no. 8 (October 1970), p. 34.

37. Quoted in Ashton, *About Rothko*, p. 174.

38. Breslin, *Mark Rothko*, p. 482.

39. In his review of the Breslin biography, *New York Times Book Review*, 2 December 1993, p. 36.

40. Ibid., p. 34.

seven

1. Henry Bettenson (ed.), *Documents of the Christian Church* (Oxford, 1963), p. 94.

2. Egon Sendler, *The Icon: Image of the Invisible – Elements of Theology, Aesthetics and Technique* (Torrance CA, 1988), pp. 187–239.

3. For Theophanes, see Olga Popova in Roderick Grierson (ed.), *Gates of Mystery: The Art of Holy Russia* (Fort Worth TX, 1993), pp. 55–8; and Robin Cormack, *Painting the Soul* (London, 1997), pp. 172–91.

4. For Rublev, see Temple, *Icons*, pp. 108–11. Tarkovsky's cinematic treatment of the artist's life and work (*Andrei Rublev*, 1966) is perceptively discussed by Mark Le Fanu in *The Films of Andrei Tarkovsky* (London, 2000), pp. 33–52.

5. The work receives perceptive theological commentary from both

George Pattison, *Art, Modernity and Faith* (London, 1991), pp. 128–31, and Rowan Williams, *The Dwelling of the Light: Praying with Icons of Christ* (Norwich, 2003), pp. 41–63.

6. Especially insightful is David Davies, 'El Greco's Religious Art', in *El Greco* (London, 2003), pp. 45–71. For the artist's pre-Spanish career, see especially Nicos Hadjinicolaou, *El Greco of Crete* (Heraklion, 1980). For the later El Greco, see Jonathan M. Brown, *Images and Ideas in Seventeenth Century Spanish Painting* (Princeton NJ 1978); Richard G. Mann, *El Greco and His Patrons* (Cambridge, 1986); and especially John Wesley Cook, 'El Greco's Art in Counter-Reformation Spain', in Doug Adams and Diane Apostolos-Cappadona (eds), *Art as Religious Studies* (New York, 1987), pp. 131–48. A contrasting cultural perspective is Victor Stoichita, *Visionary Experience in the Golden Age of Spanish Art* (London, 1995).

7. For Rembrandt, see William Halewood, *Six Subjects of Reformation Art: A Preface to Rembrandt* (Toronto, 1982). Also Arthur K. Wheelock (ed.), *Rembrandt's Late Religious Portraits* (Chicago, 2005), especially Volker Manueth, 'Rembrandt's Apostles: Pillars of Faith and Witnesses of the Word', pp. 39–55. Also Visser 't Hooft, *Rembrandt and the Gospel* (London, 1947); and Christopher Joby, 'How Does the Work of Rembrandt van Rijn Represent a Calvinist Aesthetic?', *Theology*, vol. 107, no. 835 (2004), pp. 22–9.

8. 'T Hooft, *Rembrandt*, p. 37.

9. Ibid., p. 70.

10. Joby, 'How Does the Work of Rembrandt van Rijn Represent a Calvinist Aesthetic?', p. 24.

11. William Holman Hunt, *Pre-Raphaelitism and the Pre-Raphaelite Brotherhood*, 2 vols (London, 1905). Also George P. Landow, *William Holman Hunt and Typological Symbolism* (New Haven CT, 1979); and Jeremy Maas, *Holman Hunt and the Light of the World* (London, 1984).

12. William Bell Scott, *Autobiographical Notes*, 2 vols (London 1892), Vol. II, p. 229.

13. Ibid., p. 76.

14. Hunt: *Pre-Raphaelitism*, Vol. I, p. 349.

15. Walker Art Gallery, *William Holman Hunt* (Liverpool, 1969), pp. 40–41.

16. John Ruskin, *Modern Painters*, 2nd edn (Orpington, 1898), Vol. III, pp. 186–96.

17. John Ruskin, *Academy Notes* (London, 1856), pp. 61–3.

18. For a detailed analysis and critique of the 1851 Religious Census, see Keith Snell and Paul Ell, *Rival Jerusalems: The Geography of Victorian Religion* (Cambridge, 2000), esp. chs 1, 2.

19. Bell Scott, *Autobiographical Notes*, Vol. 1, p. 312; also reprinted in Maas, *Holman Hunt*, p. 15.

eight

1. Tom Devonshire Jones and Graham Howes, *English Cathedrals and the Visual Arts: Patronage, Policies and Provision* (London, 2005) surveys the process in an Anglican context. Art and Christianity Enquiry (ACE) and Art in Sacred Places (ASP) are the two major British advisory bodies.

2. John Gage (ed.), *Goethe on Art* (Berkeley CA, 1980), p. 55.

3. Paul Tillich, *On Art and Architecture*, ed. John and Jane Dillenberger (New York, 1987), p. 207.

4. Hayum, *God's Medicine*, pp. 7–8.

5. Donald Kuspit, *The End of Art*, esp. ch. 5.

6. Martin, James, *Beauty and Holiness* (Princeton, 1990), p. 192.

7. Arthur C. Danto, *The Philosophical Disenfranchisement of Art* (New York, 1986).

8. Couturier, *Sacred Art*, p. 52.

9. Frank Burch Brown, *Religious Aesthetics* (Princeton, 1989), p. 111.

10. Otto, *The Idea of the Holy*, p. 67.

11. Hayum, *God's Medicine*, p. 117.

12. Robert Hewison, *John Ruskin: The Argument of the Eye* (London, 1976).

13. Burch Brown, *Religious Aesthetics*, pp. 185–6.

14. Rosemary Crumlin (ed.), *Beyond Belief: Modern Art and the Religious Imagination* (Melbourne, 1998), p. 9.

15. In ibid., p. 22.

16. For a useful, if uneven, appraisal of Viola's work, see Chris Townsend (ed.), *The Art of Bill Viola* (London, 2004). Also Felicity Sparrow (ed.)

Bill Viola: The Messenger (Durham, 2003); Bill Hall and David Jasper (eds), *Art and the Spiritual* (Sunderland, 2003); and David Packwood, 'Bill Viola: The Passions', in *The Art Book*, vol. 11, no. 4 (2004), pp. 8–10. Primary quotations are drawn from these sources, unless otherwise stated. I am also indebted to Peter Thorn for some valuable insights on Viola.

17. Quoted by Alan Jenkins in *Times Literary Supplement*, 28 November 2003, p. 18.

18. *Guardian*, 19 March 2002.

19. Quoted by David Morgan, in Townsend (ed.), *The Art of Bill Viola*, p. 101.

20. The best current study of Gormley is John Hutchinson et al. (eds), *Anthony Gormley*, rev. edn (London, 2000). Also Keith Walker and Simon Morley on 'Gormley's "Space, 1986"', *Art and Christianity Enquiry Bulletin* 14 (April 1998), pp. 1–3.

21. St Augustine, *Confessions* Book X.8 (15), cited in Hutchinson et al. (eds), *Anthony Gormley*, p. 111.

22. Hutchinson et al. (eds), *Anthony Gormley*, p. 28.

23. Ibid., p. 25.

24. Cited by Paul Vallely, *Independent*, 20 April 2004.

25. John Hutchinson in *Anthony Gormley*, p. 51.

26. Address to the 'Art and Spirituality' conference, Durham Cathedral, 1996, in Hall and Jasper, *Art and the Spiritual*, p. 14.

27. Ibid., p. 16.

28. A.G. Williams, *Craigie: The Art of Craigie Aitchison* (Edinburgh, 1996); Helen Lessore, *Craigie Aitchison Paintings 1953–1981* (London, 1981); Andrew Lambirth, *Craigie Aitchison: Recent Paintings* (London, 1989), and *Craigie Aitchison: Out of the Ordinary* (London, 2003). Quotations from the artist himself are drawn from these sources.

29. Lambirth, *Craigie Aitchison: Out of the Ordinary*, p. 15.

30. Max Weber, *Essays on Art* (Los Angeles, 1912), p. 33.

nine

1. Jacques Ellul, *The Technological Society* (London, 1965).

2. Erwin Panofsky, *Gothic Architecture and Scholasticism* (New York, 1957).

3. Gerth and Wright Mills (eds), *From Max Weber*, p. 342.

4. Morse Peckham, *Romanticism and Behaviour: Collected Essays*, 2 vols (Durham NC, 1957), vol. 2, pp. 94–5.

5. Peter Berger and Thomas Luckmann, *The Social Reality of Religion* (London, 1969). For a useful critique of their position, see Linda Woodhead (ed.), *Peter Berger and the Study of Religion* (London, 2001).

6. See especially his *Theoria: Art and the Absence of Grace* (London, 1988).

7. Morgan, *Visual Piety, passim*.

8. Tillich, *Theology of Culture*, p. 74

9. John Berger, *Ways of Seeing* (London, 1972).

10. George Steiner, *Real Presences* (London, 1989), pp. 229–31.

11. John Dillenberger, *A Theology of Artistic Sensibilities* (London, 1986), pp. 215–28.

12. Karl Barth, *Wolfgang Amadeus Mozart* (Grand Rapids MI, 1986), pp. 33–40, 55–7.

13. Karl Barth, 'The Architectural Problem of Protestant Places of Worship', in A. Bieler (ed.), *Archtecture and Worship* (Edinburgh and London, 1965), p. 93.

14. Otto, *The Idea of the Holy*, p. 70.

15. Paul Tillich, 'On the Theology of Fine Art and Architecture', in *On Art and Architecture*, p. 207.

16. Ibid., p. 219.

17. Ibid., p. 80.

18. Ibid., p. 113.

19. Ibid., p. 124; stress added.

20. Ibid., p. xxv.

21. See David Jasper, 'Untitled: Theology and American Abstract Expressionism', *Religious Studies and Theology*, April 1995, pp. 21–35.

22. Karl Rahner, 'Theology and the Arts', *Thought: Fordham University Quarterly* 57 (1982), from which all the direct quotations from Rahner are taken.

23. Ray Hart, *Unfinished Man and the Imagination* (New York, 1979), p. 19.

24. John Cobb, *Christ in a Pluralistic Age* (Philadelphia, 1975), pp. 42–3.

25. Kung, *Art and the Question of Meaning*, p. 52.

26. Mark C. Taylor, *Disfiguring* (Chicago, 1992), p. 114.

27. Nicholas Wolterstorff, *Art in Action: Toward a Christian Aesthetic* (Grand Rapids MI, 1980), p. 169.

28. Burch Brown, *Religious Aesthetics*, p. 17. Balthasar's *The Glory of the Lord: A Theological Aesthetics* (San Francisco, 1982–90), 7 vols, is his magnum opus. The first volume is the most immediately accessible for the general reader.

29. Burch Brown, *Religious Aesthetics*, p. 158.

30. Flanagan, *Seen and Unseen*, p. 16.

31. Michael Camille, *The Gothic Idol: Ideology and Image-Making in Medieval Art* (Cambridge, 1989), p. 347.

select bibliography

Each preceding chapter and its accompanying endnotes already contain many specific bibliographical references. What follows below is intended both to supplement these and to direct readers towards other dimensions of the relationship between religion and the visual arts not specifically engaged with in the text itself. The two asterisked items contain wide-ranging and useful bibliographies of their own.

Adams, Doug, and Diana Apostolos-Cappadona (eds) (1987) *Art in Religious Studies* (New York: Crossroad).

Adams, Henry (1981) *Mont St Michel and Chartres* (Princeton: Princeton University Press).

Apostolos-Cappadona, Diana (ed.) (1995) *Art, Creativity and the Sacred*, rev. edn (New York: Continuum).*

Baxendall, Michael (1960) *Giotto and the Orators* (Oxford: Clarendon Press).

Belting, Hans (1994) *Likeness and Presence: A History of the Image Before the Era of Art* (Chicago: Chicago University Press).

Besancon, Alain (2000) *The Forbidden Image: An Intellectual History of Iconoclasm* (Chicago: Chicago University Press).

Binski, Paul (2005) *Becket's Crown: Art and Imagination in Gothic England, 1170–1300* (New Haven and London: Yale University Press).

Brandon, S.G.F. (1975) *Man and God in Art and Ritual* (New York: Charles Scribner's Sons).

Brown Burch, Frank (2000) *Good Taste, Bad Taste and Christian Taste* (Oxford: Oxford University Press).

Burckhardt, Titus (1976) *Art of Islam: Language and Meaning* (Westerham: World of Islam Festival Publishing).

Christensen, Carl G. (1979) *Art and the Reformation in Germany* (Athens: Ohio University Press).

De Gruchy, John W. (2001) *Christianity, Art and Transformation: Theological Aesthetics in the Struggle for Justice* (Cambridge: Cambridge University Press).

Dixon, John W. (1980) *Art and the Theological Imagination* (New York: Seabury Press).

——— (1994) *The Christ of Michaelangelo* (Atlanta GA: Scholars Press).

——— (1996) *Images of Truth: Religion and the Art of Seeing* (Atlanta GA: Scholars Press).

Eire, Carlos (1986) *War Against the Idols* (Cambridge: Cambridge University Press).

Elkins, James (2004) *On the Strange Place of Religion in Contemporary Art* (London and New York: Routledge).

Eyck, Diana L. (1981) *Darsan: Seeing the Divine Image in India* (Chambersburg PA: Anima Books).

Fuller, Peter (1985) *Images of God: The Consolations of Lost Illusions* (London, Chatto & Windus).

Freedberg, David (1989) *The Power of Images: Studies in the History and Theory of Response* (Chicago: University of Chicago Press).

Gutmann, Joseph (ed.) (1977) *The Image and the Word: Confrontations in Judaism, Christianity and* Islam (Missoula MN: Scholars Press).

Grabar, Andre (1968) *Christian Iconography: A Study of its Origins* (Princeton NJ: Princeton University Press).

Grabar, Oleg (1987) *The Formation of Islamic Art*, rev. edn (New Haven CT: Yale University Press).

Hall, Marcia (ed.) (2005) *Michelangelo's Last Judgement* (Cambridge: Cambridge University Press).

Hackett, Rosalind I. (1996) *Art and Religion in Africa* (London: Cassell).

Heller Giurescu, Ena (ed.) (2004) *Reluctant Partners: Art and Religion in Dialogue* (New York: Bible Society).*

Hinnells, John (1990) 'Religion and the Arts', in Ursula King (ed.), *Turning Points in Religious Studies: Essays in Honour of Geoffrey Parrinder* (Edinburgh: T. & T. Clark).

Hornstein, Shelley, et al. (2003) *Impossible Images: Contemporary Art after the Holocaust* (New York and London: New York University Press).

Jensen, Robin M. (2004) *The Substance of Things Seen: Art, Faith, and the Christian Community* (Grand Rapids MI: Eerdmans).

Jopling, Carol F. (1971) *Art and Aesthetics in Primitive Societies* (New York: Dutton).

Kandinsky, Wassily (1977) *Concerning the Spiritual in Art* (New York: Dover).

Lipsey, Roger (2004) *The Spiritual in Twentieth Century Art* (Mineola NY: Dover).

Mango, Cyril (ed.) (1986) *The Art of the Byzantine Empire 312–1453: Sources and Documents* (Toronto: University of Toronto Press).

Malraux, André (1954) *The Voices of Silence*, trans. Stuart Gilbert (London: Secker).

———— (1960) *The Metamorphosis of the Gods*, trans. Stuart Gilbert (Garden City NY: Doubleday).

Martland, Thomas R. (1981) *Religion as Art: An Interpretation* (Albany NY: SUNY Press).

Miles, Margaret (1985) *Image as Insight: Visual Understanding in Western Christianity and Secular Culture* (Boston MA: Beacon Press).

Monti, Anthony (2003) *A Natural Theology of the Arts* (Aldershot: Ashgate).

Moore, Albert C. (1977) *Iconography of World Religions: An Introduction* (Philadelphia: Fortress).

———— (1995) *Arts in the Religions of the Pacific: Symbols of Life* (London: Pinter).

Mormando, Franco (ed.) (1999) *Saints and Sinners: Caravaggio and the Baroque Image* (Chicago: University of Chicago Press).

Nichols, Aidan (1980) *The Art of God Incarnate: Theology and Symbol from Genesis to the Twentieth Century* (London: Darton, Longman & Todd).

Norman, Diana (ed.) (1995) *Siena, Florence and Padua: Art, Society, Religion 1280–1400*, 2 vols (New Haven CT: Yale University Press).

Norman, Edward (1990) *The House of God: Church Architecture, Style and History* (London: Thames & Hudson).

Ousterhout R., and L. Brubaker (1994) *The Sacred Image: East and West*

(Urbana IL: University of Illinois Press).

Paine, Crispin (ed.) (2000) *Godly Things: Museum, Objects and Religion* (London: Leicester University Press).

Palmer, Michael F. (1988) *Paul Tillich's Philosophy of Art* (Berlin: de Gruyter).

Panofsky, Erwin (1946) *Abbot Suger on the Abbey Church of St Denis* (Princeton: Princeton University Press).

———— (1957) *Gothic Architecture and Scholasticism* (New York: Meridian).

Pilgrim, Richard B. (1993) *Buddhism and the Arts of Japan* (New York: Dover).

Rawson, Phillip (1967) *The Art of Southeast Asia* (London: Thames & Hudson).

Rookmaaker, Hans R. (1994) *Modern Art and the Death of a Culture* (Leicester: Apollos).

Sherry, Patrick (1992) *Spirit and Beauty: An Introduction to Theological Aesthetics* (Oxford: Oxford University Press).

———— (2003) *Images of Redemption: Art, Literature and Salvation* (Edinburgh: T. & T. Clark).

Thiessen, Gesa E. (2004) *Theological Aesthetics: A Reader* (London: SCM Press).

Van der Leeuw, Gerardus (1963) *Sacred and Profane Beauty: The Holy in Art* (London: Weidenfeld).

Van Os, Henk (1994) *The Art of Devotion in the Later Middle Ages in Europe 1300–1500* (Princeton NJ: Princeton University Press).

Verdon, Timothy, and John Henderson (eds) (1990) *Christianity and the Renaissance: Image and Imagination in the Quattrocento* (Syracuse NY: Syracuse University Press).

journals

Religion and the Arts (Boston MA: Boston College).

ARTS: The Arts in Religious and Theological Studies (Minneapolis/St Paul: United Theological Seminary).

Art and Christianity (London: ACE).

Material Religion (Oxford: Berg).